Ellen White: Friend of Angels

Stories from her amazing adventures, travels, and relationships

Paul B. Ricchiuti

Pacific Press® Publishing Association
Nampa, Idaho
Oshawa, Ontario, Canada

Edited by B. Russell Holt
Designed by Tim Larson
Cover illustration by Marcus Mashburn

Copyright © 1999 by
Pacific Press® Publishing Association
Printed in the United States of America
All Rights Reserved

Accuracy of all quotations and references is the responsibility of
the author.

Ricchiuti, Paul B.
    Ellen White : friend of angels : stories from her amazing
adventures, travels, and relationships / Paul B. Ricchiuti.
        p.   cm.
    Includes bibliographical references.
    ISBN 0-8163-1707-0 (pbk. : alk. paper)
    1. White, Ellen Gould Harmon, 1827-1915. 2. Seventh-day
Adventists—United States—Biography. I. Title.
BX6193.@5R51   1999
286.7'092—dc21   98-47469
    [B]   CIP

99 00 01 02 03 • 5 4 3 2 1

Dedication

To the memory of
Arthur L. White,
a true and faithful friend.

Contents

Foreword

More than a century and a half has passed since the Great Disappointment of 1844. William Miller and those expecting the Lord's return in that year have long passed from the scene. Yet that one event, so desperately and yearningly looked for, is still anticipated in the hearts of countless millions today. They want the Lord to come. Ellen White dedicated her every breath to hastening that event. Also tied to this "blessed hope" was her fundamental belief in the seventh-day Sabbath and the three angels' messages. This was what she lived for. Her life was filled with adventure, bitter frustrations, and an ongoing war with Satan of which even close friends were unaware.

But now Ellen White is gone. She is not forgotten, however, for her writings—writings she so carefully and painfully produced at great personal cost—are ever with us. Most of these writings, sad to say, stand side by side in row after row of dusty, beautifully bound books. They wait patiently, unopened on shelves, in the homes of most Seventh-day Adventists, waiting to be read or re-read.

Although the days of Ellen White's life are over and her time has passed, that should make no difference, for from the dried ink of her pen still springs the joyful message of a warm, loving, and soon-to-appear God. She gave her life to bear this message. Among her final words, she whispered, "I know in Whom I have believed."

By writing this book, it is my intention to show just a little of how God used His faithful messenger. This book will also attempt to tell the effect Ellen White had on the people of her day—and continues to have on people today.

Visions? Oh yes, she had them. Yet you will find no explanation for them here. That subject has been carefully researched and discussed by others. Their work is readily available in other volumes. Some of those visions, however, will be referred to now and then as this book progresses, as the need for them arises.

So let's begin now on a trip through time, to a day and age that still reaches out to touch us in our busy, modern lives. It is time to take yet another look at this remarkable little woman and the world she lived in.

Paul B. Ricchiuti
Nampa, Idaho

Introduction

Shadows crawled across the grounds of an ancient house. Like unseen giants they reached out covering everything they touched. The wind twisted trees and snapped their branches back and forth in the dark. It pounded them against the sides of that dark, old building. Leaves knifed through the air like weapons, scraping and clawing on windowpanes.

But all was silent inside the house. Nothing moved. Hallways were deathly still; door after door remained closed. No light appeared anywhere. Then, very faint and far off, almost lost against the screaming storm, came a slow, steady squeaking sound. It came from a slowly opening door, being pushed out wider and wider into a hall. Then the door stopped moving, and everything was still again in the old house. But something, or someone, had entered the hall.

There was no light, only a blur of misty white. Then the object began to move. It seemed to float. On and on it went, passing door after closed door. Then it stopped at the end of the hall facing a heavy, solid door, closed as were the others. But this door was different. A faint glow of light crept from the space beneath its huge frame.

The shadowy figure in the hall bent forward, revealing itself to be a small child. It was a girl in a long white nightdress. Slowly and with caution, she gently placed an ear next to the door. She tensed as she listened. Then a smile crossed her face, and her eyes sparkled brightly at what she heard. Someone was singing on the other side of the door. The voice was soft and quiet, almost like a hum.

The girl knew who was behind that door. It was Grandma. She stood smiling as she listened. Then the song ended, and there was silence. The little girl backed away; on quiet tiptoes she ran down the long hall and rushed to her room.

The wind played its wild tricks as the storm continued. There was moaning and scraping on the roof. But the girl, snuggled in her warm little bed, slept a happy, contented sleep. And there was a smile on her face.

But the light, the one coming from beneath the door at the end of the hall, continued until dawn. Then, and only then, did it go out.

Why did a small girl leave her warm bed in the middle of the night just to listen for sounds coming from behind a closed door?

The girl was named Ella, and she had listened at Grandma's door many times. "Sometimes," she said, "I would slip out of my cot . . . see a glimmer of light coming from Grandma's room, or hear her footsteps on the floor. . . . I knew," she continued, "that she was writing, writing as fast as her pen could go."[1]

Ella's grandmother was Ellen White, and there was a deep love between the two. Ella realized her grandmother was special. She also knew that she was writing down the messages God had given her. They were for God's people on earth. Some people called Grandma a prophet of God. Others, even Ellen herself, said she was just God's messenger. And Ella was wise enough not to interrupt Grandma while she was doing God's work.

In 1895, near Cooranbong, Australia, Ella and Ellen shared a tent while Grandma's house was being built. Ella tells about it. "Sometimes I was awakened in the small hours of the morning by the light from her kerosene lamp, and I drew aside the curtain that partitioned my corner from the rest of the tent, peeked out, and saw her writing, bolstered up in bed with pillows or sitting in an easy chair with a lapboard across her knees. Her usual time for rising was three o'clock, often earlier."[2] Another time, Ella wrote: "One of my chief delights was to slip away . . . and steal quietly into Grandma's room. Without lifting her eyes from the page, she would bid me come in. I knew better than to interrupt her writing and would wait silently until she laid down her pen and looked up. This was the signal for one of those delightful little chats that I loved so much."[3]

Let's turn now to the summer of 1870. The scene is far different, yet in some ways it is similar. We see Ellen, her husband, James, and their son Willie on a Mississippi riverboat. They have boarded as passengers at Dubuque, Iowa.

Sailing on the Mississippi was more than delightful; it was a real pleasure. But as the others enjoyed the ride, for Ellen, it was different. Once on board, she located a small table, spread her papers on it, and began to write. James expressed his feelings when he wrote: "The day was very hot, Mrs. W. is writing [he often referred to his wife as Mrs. W]. Poor woman! This almost eternal writing . . . when she should rest, and enjoy the beautiful scenery and the pleasant society, seems too bad."[4] James was alone with Willie and a boat full of strangers while Ellen was off in a corner writing.

Later that day, a passenger asked James if his wife was a public speaker. James answered "Yes." The news got around, and some of the passengers started talking about her. They urged James to ask Ellen if she would speak to the passengers.

James knew where to find her. And, sure enough, she was at the same small table, "still busy writing."[5] James told her of the passengers' request, and she finally said she would be happy to talk to them. It turned out to be a pleasant experience.

Whatever she was doing or wherever she was, Ellen often found herself fighting lonely battles against Satan and his evil powers. She never forgot, however, that she had special help from God Himself. He was her guide. She knew that well, for her trust was always in Him.

Many of Ellen's battlefields were on paper. She fought hard and bitter conflicts with a pen. Few human beings, even today, could shape, guide, and plan for the future of God's church on earth as she did. Her writings have altered the lives of hundreds of thousands who look for the soon coming of our Lord and Savior Jesus Christ.

Now let's pause for a closer and deeper look into Ellen White's personality and her motivation to write.

We turn first to *Selected Messages*, book 1. Ellen wrote: "I am to bear the message that is given me to bear, so long as the Lord shall choose. . . . The Lord has said to me: 'Bear the testimonies. Your work is not to settle difficulties; your work is to reprove, and to present the righteousness of Christ.' "[6]

"My writings are kept on file in the office, and even though I should not live, these words that have been given to me by the Lord will still have life and will speak to the people."[7]

We turn now to another of Mrs. White's books, *Testimonies for the Church*, volume 5: "I have been aroused from my sleep with a vivid sense of subjects previously presented to my mind; and I have written, at midnight, letters that have gone across the continent and, arriving at a crisis, have saved great disaster to the cause of God. This has been my work for many years."[8]

After a low point in her life, when she was tempted to doubt her work and question her role with God, she wrote: "I did not realize that I was unfaithful in thus questioning and doubting, and did not see the danger and sin of such a course, until in vision I was taken into the presence of Jesus. He looked upon me with a frown, and turned His face from me. It is not possible to describe the terror and agony I then felt. I fell upon my face before Him, but had no power to utter a word. . . . The angel raised me to my feet, and said: . . . 'If you are faithful to the end, you shall eat of the tree of life, and shall drink of the river of the water of life. You will have to suffer much, but the grace of God is sufficient.' I then felt willing to do all that the Lord might require me to do."[9]

Again, in her own words: "Said the angel: . . . 'Deliver the message faithfully; endure unto the end, and you shall eat the fruit of the tree of life and drink from the water of life.' "[10]

That angel promise, however, is not the entire story, nor is it the basic reason for all her writing. The angel, who appeared to Ellen in hundreds of visions and dreams, emphasized a few key words along with the promise. Two of these words were *endure* and *faithfully*. To deliver God's messages *faithfully* was not easy. There was often terrible opposition to what she wrote and preached, especially from church members themselves. She also faced intense unbelief, even from her friends, right up to the end of her life. To faithfully endure under such conditions took tremendous strength.

The well-known and much-loved Adventist radio evangelist, H. M. S. Richards, Sr., once told me, "If you want something done, get a short person to do it." He went on to add that people like Napoleon and Ellen White (who stood only a little over five feet tall) often did powerful things.

Yet even after reading the explanations Ellen gave for her writings, we still have not yet found the complete answer to our question: Why did Ellen White do all that exhaustive, time-consuming writing?

The answer is very simple. She was in love with God and wanted to please Him. And she wanted very much for others to experience that same love. That's all it was.

1. Ella M. Robinson, "Early Recollections of My Grandmother," *The Youth's Instructor*, March 16, 1948.

2. Ella M. Robinson, "Later Recollections of My Grandmother," *The Youth's Instructor*, March 23, 1948.

3. Ella M. Robinson, "Early Recollections of My Grandmother," *The Youth's Instructor*, March 16, 1948.

4. Spirit of Prophecy Emphasis Week (workbook) (Washington, D.C.: The Ellen G. White Estate, 1972), 24.

5. Ibid.

6. *Selected Messages*, 1:52, 53.

7. Ibid., 55.

8. *Testimonies for the Church*, 5:65.

9. *Life Sketches*, 90, 91.

10. *Christian Experience and Teachings of Ellen White*, 1:68.

CHAPTER ONE

Night in a Locked Room

F or Ellen White, 1890 was an exceptionally busy year. At home in Battle Creek, Michigan, there were meetings, speaking appointments, people to see, letters to write—and there were books to be written. The church was growing faster with each passing day.

But with growth came problems. The church seemed to be spinning out of control as the message spread in all directions. Church members, even church leaders, were fighting among themselves. Grudges led to disunity; there was jealousy.

What could be done about it? This was the nagging question on Ellen's heart. She knew that these personal fires had to be put out.

Let's take a look at a few of the problems facing the church at that time. As we do, we can only wonder how one small woman could possibly cope with all she was facing. She was not alone in her fight, of course. She never was. God was her Friend, and He would guide her as He always did. But before we look at the problems in the world of Seventh-day Adventists, let's look at what was going on that year in the larger world—the world in which Ellen White lived at the beginning of the last decade of the nineteenth century.

According to the census of 1890, the population of the United States was 62,947,214. The figure had doubled from the days just prior to the American Civil War. In the ten years since 1880, there had been an increase of 12.8 million people. Immigrants—mostly from Europe—accounted for some 5 million of that number. More than a third of the population of the country lived in cities.

Women were coming into their own; 3.7 million of them joined the working class. Wyoming became the first state in the nation to give women the vote. Hull House, the facility Jane Adams established in downtown Chicago to help the poor and downtrodden, was in full swing. At the other end of the spectrum, Marshall Field's department store in Chicago boasted an annual sales total of 35 million dollars. Its slogan, aimed at women buyers, was: "Give the lady what she wants." It paid off.

In those days, children suffered hardships that we can hardly imagine today. An estimated 603,000 boys and girls between the ages of ten and fourteen worked long days in physically demanding jobs for small wages.

But overall, optimism was high. "If you believe it, make it happen" was a general attitude. And people across America were doing just that. Frank Lloyd Wright hit the construction world by storm with his new concept in home building. Wright had the idea of building a house that would blend into the site, making it looking like a part of the landscape. His designs were revolutionary and made him famous. Buildings became taller and taller. People began calling them "skyscrapers."

Thirty-year-old William Jennings Bryan was elected to congress. Railroads were replacing cowboys and their long cattle drives. Congress passed the Anti-Trust Act aimed at monopolies and big business. On July 3, 1890, Idaho became the forty-third state, with Boise as its capital. Wyoming followed with statehood on July 10. Yellowstone became the nation's first national park on September 25. That same year the United Mine Workers was formed as a labor union, and Congress created the Oklahoma Territory.

The list could go on and on. The first Army-Navy football game took place (final score: Navy 24, Army 0). In the entertainment world, Buffalo Bill came along with his Wild West Show, outdoing even the great showman, Barnum, himself.

Strong family ties held the nation together. Henry Ford summed up the prevailing thinking when he said, "More than once I've heard mother say, 'If we can't be happy here in this house, we'd never be happy anywhere.'"

Booker T. Washington, a black educator and friend of the powerful, became a national figure. He was tall, muscular, and commanded attention with his piercing eyes. He could hold a crowd in the palm of his hand and bring the people to their feet cheering in seconds. He stressed honesty, hard work, thrift, and cleanliness. He urged his students to be polite and obey the laws. He believed Blacks should develop vocational skills. "I would set no limits," he said, "to the attainments of the Negro in arts, letters, or statesmanship. And I believe," he continued, "the surest way to reach those ends is by laying the foundation in the little things of life that lie immediately about one's door."

Doesn't this sound much like something Ellen White herself might have said?

Finally, in 1890 a Sioux brave named Wovoka reported he had seen visions that told him the white man would soon go to another world, leaving the red man to his former lands. The news spread like wildfire; Sioux tribes gathered in large numbers to await the great day. Dances sprung up; they were called "Ghost Dances" and caused fear in the hearts of Whites.

Army troops were sent to the Pine Ridge Indian Agency in South Dakota. The Indians fled. Then on December 15, 1890, Chief Sitting Bull and a delegation of Indians tried to calm the situation. Sitting Bull was arrested; a fight broke out, and when it was over the great chief lay dead. Clashes and fighting followed, leading to a great slaughter of Indians at Wounded Knee. Savage fighting continued for several weeks until the last major outbreak of hostilities between the white man and Indian came to an end.

There we have a synopsis of the momentous events of 1890. "But," one might ask, "what does all this have to do with Ellen White?"

Ellen was well aware of the events going on in the world around her, but she had more important matters on her mind. The salvation of souls and the advancement of God's cause overruled all else. She was engaged in a war of her own, and she knew how to go about fighting it. Let's look in on this little lady and her warfare against the enemies of God.

At home in Battle Creek during 1890, she kept four workers busy on different kinds of books. "This with my much letter writing", she wrote, "seems to keep me employed from 3:00 a.m. till 7:00 p.m."[1]

In February and March she was busy with a twenty-week ministerial institute held in the Battle Creek Tabernacle Church. During a series of early morning talks, she became aware that something was wrong. She sensed resentment, distrust, and bad feelings aimed at her. The historic 1888 General Conference Session lay only two years in the past and was still in the minds of many. Grudges still lived on in the hearts of several who had been delegates to that session and who had experienced firsthand the crisis that had come to the church then. One individual, an Elder Larson, wrote Ellen White a note in which he asked her to publicly confess that she had been wrong to sharply rebuke him in Minneapolis two years earlier.

What was her reaction? "This matter sunk my heart like lead," she wrote. "What to say to these men, how to treat their strong spirits, was a difficult problem to solve. I knew not what to do. I knew that the Lord urged me to give the testimony [to Elder Larson] that I did."[2]

Ellen continued with her morning talks at the ministerial institute, but it wasn't easy. In spite of the tensions, however, word began getting around about the excellent talks Ellen was giving. People were telling each other, "Don't miss them." Many were blessed as they crowded in each morning. Soon well over three hundred persons filled the east vestry of the tabernacle. Some of these early morning meetings lasted two hours! Ellen's topics were simple, centering on faith and God's love.

There had been great misunderstandings in 1888, and the bad feelings lingered. Some still suspected their fellow church members of making plans to push through strange, new doctrines under the guise of new light. Tensions ran high, yet through it all Ellen remained calm, trusting God and doing His will.

In the foreword to her book *Testimonies to Ministers and Gospel Workers,* we find these words: "Unfortunately, several among the leaders of our work connected with the General Conference and our institutions at Battle Creek ranked themselves on the negative side and established in the very heart of the work of the church a hard core of resistance."[3]

Leaders in the Seventh-day Adventist Church were looking suspiciously at Ellen White and her work. Ministers and church workers were divided, especially over the reliability of Ellen White's testimonies and the basis for her writings. Some didn't believe the testimonies at all, yet they continued to sit each morning and listen to her as she spoke.

"I am convinced," wrote Ellen, "that Satan saw that there was very much at stake here, and he did not want to lose his hold on our ministering brethren."[4]

On March 10, Ellen answered a letter she had received from

Elder Canard. He was one who questioned her work, and in his letter he raised a number of issues. In her answer to him, she wrote: "Your question I will answer as best I can. I take no credit of ability in myself to write the articles in the paper or to write the books which I publish. Certainly I could not originate them. I have been receiving light for the last forty-five years and I have been communicating the light given me of heaven to our people as well as to all whom I could reach. I am seeking to do the will of my heavenly Father."[5]

But all the stress and resentments were starting to tell on Ellen. She was beginning to crack. She thought of giving up. But as she reflected, she stated, "The Lord has made known to me [that] I must stand at my post of duty and [that] He would stand by me."[6]

No, she didn't give up. But in a letter to her son Willie she confessed, "I have never passed through such a scene of conflict, such determined resistance to the truth—the light that God has been pleased to give me—as since the Minneapolis meeting."[7] "Willie," she wrote, "I talked as they had never heard me talk before."[8]

What was the outcome of all this? Did God stand by her?

As Ellen continued with her morning talks at the ministerial institute, she noticed that some who had doubted her and her work were slowly changing their minds. God was indeed at work. She mentions a few of these by name: Olds, Grighouse, Warren, Fero, Watt, and Olsen. "Many," she commented, "whose names I do not know are coming into the light."[9]

There were others, however, who were not changing their minds. Elder Larson was one of these. She wondered about his case and that of others. "What course Dan Jones may take now and what course Porter and Larson will take, who have been so actively engaged in sowing their unbelief and prejudice, I cannot imagine." Then she added (and one can almost hear her saying it),

"I hope they will be born again."[10]

Ellen White's position on the subject of righteousness by faith is found in her book, *Testimonies to Ministers and Gospel Workers*. The foreword to that book says, "She [Ellen White] spoke of this Bible truth [righteousness by faith] as one which, though 'new to many minds,' was in reality 'old truth in new framework.' "[11]

In a letter to Willie, started on March 10 and finished the next day, she said, "Brother Porter [at the meeting on the morning of March 11] was on his feet all broken up. . . . He confessed to me his wrong that he had done to me. . . . He humbly asked us to forgive him . . . said he had been disbelieving the testimonies, but he said, 'I believe them now.' " The letter goes on: "Brother Larson . . . spoke and confessed to me, confessed his feelings had not been right. I responded and he took his position on the testimonies."

She also noted in her letter that "Brother Dan Jones was present. He kept his head bowed upon the seat all the time."

Elder O. A. Olsen who presided over the institute "wept like a baby," said Ellen White, "when brother Larson and Porter were on their feet." In another part of her letter to Willie she wrote, "The whole room was sobbing and praising God." "The Spirit of God is at work," she concluded, and there was real evidence that indeed He was.

At these early morning meetings, Ellen fought with everything she had. Lives were at stake, lives for whom Jesus had died. Lives that Satan was trying to tear away from God. And Ellen knew it. But now she was tired and completely worn out. It had been exhausting work for her; the stress had been great. "My strength is about exhausted," she said, "If it is possible, I want to get away before the last atom of strength shall be gone here."[12]

After these events in Battle Creek, Ellen White spent much of the rest of 1890 traveling. Weary and full of stress as she was, she was ready to do her duty. The little lady packed her bags. We watch her now in a small locked compartment of a railway car as she heads across the American West. Leaving Battle Creek behind with all its difficult days, she may not realize it, but difficult days lie ahead as well, even great, devastating fires, but these are matters for another day and another time.

Her schedule was Chicago, then Colorado, California, back to Colorado, and finally Battle Creek once more.

She stayed in Chicago only for a weekend. Not much evidence remained of the great fire that had leveled much of the city nineteen years before. More than two hundred fifty people had been killed, and 90,000 were left homeless. But Chicago had rebuilt and was running well again.

The main reason for Ellen to stop in Colorado was to visit her son Willie and his family. Mary, Willie's wife, was fighting a losing battle with tuberculosis.

In California, her time was spent mostly in Oakland, St. Helena, and Fresno, where she attended a camp meeting. These appointments took most of the months of April and May. June found Ellen White back in Colorado. Mary was failing fast and died on June 18 at the age of thirty-three. Her funeral was held on Wednesday, June 25, in Battle Creek.

By now, Ellen's energy was almost gone. Friends urged her to rest. She finally listened to them and went to northern Michigan in July, staying in the summer resort town of Petosky, along the shore of Lake Michigan. But even there Ellen couldn't really slow down. She planned future trips to camp meetings and then a tour through the East and South. The newly organized Atlantic Conference was asking her to come; to do so would mean work in New York City, Long Island, New Jersey, Delaware, Maryland, and the District of Columbia. It also meant appointments in Virginia and in Salamanca, New York, on the Pennsylvania-New York border.

Ellen remained in Petosky until mid-October. It was a two-month stay that rejuvenated her energies. On her return to Battle Creek she had just enough time to prepare for her three-month trip through the eastern United States and on into the south.[13]

At 11 o'clock, Thursday night, October 30, 1890, Ellen White, Willie, and her companion Sara McEnterfer arrived in Salamanca, New York. The three had left Battle Creek on October 9. On one part of the trip they had traveled by boat from Boston to New York City. Ellen caught a cold upon arrival, and it didn't help her situation one bit when she had to ride the elevated trains in the city late at night. She grew worse, so the party stayed overnight. By the time they reached Salamanca, Ellen was much worse. She was tired, sick, and very nervous. The group had traveled all day by train, and now, as they got off at Salamanca, it was snowing.

Church members had great plans for her during her visit, much of it consisting of speaking appointments. She wrote in her diary: "The cold is very severe upon me. I shall attempt to speak, but it will be with difficulty."

After speaking, she returned to her diary. "The Lord did indeed help and strengthen and bless me in speaking to the people, dwelling largely upon the necessity of faith and love for one another as followers of Christ, which [and this is an enlightening comment] has been almost extinct in our churches."[14]

She spoke in the local opera house on Sunday, but her sickness was growing worse. She began to grow weak and had to be helped to the speaker's stand. The place was crowded, and Ellen talked for more than an hour.

On Monday, her head hurt and her ears were so plugged she could hardly hear her own voice. And she could stand only with difficulty.

One thing about this woman becomes clear to anyone who studies her life. No matter what difficulty she might face, she always put God and His work first. She did so again, here in Salamanca. She promised to speak the next evening, God helping her. And she did.

But Ellen was so ill by this time that she couldn't even remember afterward what she had talked about. Her diary contains this note: "Many [at the meeting that evening] spoke of the help they received from the words spoken."[15] She gave God all the credit.

By this time Ellen was desperately sick. She was staying in the home of a family named Hicks. When she arrived there after speaking that evening, someone was waiting to talk with her! An old woman wanted to discuss problems she was having with her husband. She talked at length for an hour. Ellen kindly listened through the long monologue. Then, at last, the woman left.

Weak and dangerously ill, Ellen slowly climbed the stairs to her room. Her mind was confused. But when she reached the room and closed the door, she was alone with God. She knew He would help her. Then, as she knelt by her bed, even before she could say a word, something strange and wonderful happened. She noticed a strong smell of roses. Looking up, she saw that the entire room was bathed in a soft silver light. She was instantly healed of her illness. Then she was in vision. It was November 3, 1890. Her diary entry for the next day reads in part: "What a night that was to my soul!"[16]

The next morning Willie White and A. T. Robinson were called to her room. They went, but they were slow about doing it, as they weren't sure what to expect when they got there. They anticipated the worst, expecting to have to rush her back to Battle Creek for help at the sanitarium.

Ellen was sitting in a chair when they entered the room. To their amazement, she quickly got up and greeted them with a smile. She was all aglow as she told them what had happened the night before. She was so thrilled, she said, that she hadn't been able to sleep the rest of the night! She told them an angel had appeared at the foot of her bed and told her, "Satan is your destroyer, but I am your Restorer."[17]

She went on to tell how she had been given vital information

about conditions in Battle Creek, mainly at the General Conference. All excited, she said she wanted to tell them all about what
she had been told in vision. "I seemed to be in Battle Creek," she
began, "and I was taken to the Review and Herald building, and
the angel messenger bade me, 'Follow me!'"[18]

Suddenly she stopped her story, and a strange look came over
her face. She had forgotten the rest of the vision. Confused, she
tried again to tell what she had seen and heard, but after the words
"Follow me" her mind became blank. She tried again—with the
same results. And again. The vision had been erased. Confused
and puzzled, Ellen changed the subject and began to discuss plans
for the rest of her trip.

I would like to stop our story for just a minute at this point to
add a little note about Ellen's experience a few days later when
she was traveling through New York City. The date was November
26, 1890. You will remember that she had been healed at Salamanca
by the angel. So the following will show not only how well and
strong she was following that miraculous encounter but the great
amount of energy it took for her to travel even under normal conditions.

We have the following in her own words. She, Sara
McEnterfer, and a man by the name of Miles were leaving Brook-
lyn, New York, to board a boat to Norwich, Connecticut. "We first
took a streetcar as far as the bridge," Ellen wrote, "then we climbed
the stairs to the elevated railroad [elevated trains usually ran at
about the level of a second-story building], then down the stairs
after we crossed the bridge. We were on the crowded street of
Broadway, dodging this way and then that way between teams [of
horses pulling wagons], narrowly escaping being run over. We
reached a car [a horse-drawn streetcar] we wished to take, and it
went very slowly, being obstructed with heavily loaded vehicles.
Changed cars again and just as we were about to get on board a
horsecar, there came a heavily loaded wagon drawn by two pow-

erful horses. They almost collided with the streetcar and became fixed for a time onto the car. I saw a place where we could dodge past the team and board the train [the elevated railway]. I ran, calling the others to follow with the baggage, which they did, and once more we were moving along. Soon we were obstructed with heavily laden wagons. As we were near the wharf, we decided to leave the car and walk; it was only a few rods [a rod is equal to sixteen and a half feet]. We were able, after going before teams and behind them and between them, to pass down the gangplank into the boat."[19]

And what did she do once she was on board? "Here I am writing," she says, "sitting in my berth in my stateroom."

But even that was not the end of her travel problems. She and her companions had not escaped the rush-hour traffic of New York City, on foot with their luggage, just to enjoy the quiet and peace of an all-night ride on a boat. Oh no! The adventure continued.

"At one o'clock [a.m.] the boat stopped. Then to our sorrow we learned that the gangway where all the luggage or freight was laden and unloaded was directly beneath our stateroom. There was noise of trundling wheelbarrows, orders being given, and the loading of barrels until morning. A very poor chance to sleep! We were to be awakened at four o'clock but our awakening commenced at one o'clock and continued until four."

And what happened when the boat docked?

"We must take the cars [train] at five o'clock," she wrote. "It was bitterly cold, yet beautifully pleasant. We walked quite a distance to the depot. There was a large waiting room—one room for men and women. Cards were hanging on the walls saying, 'No Smoking in This Room,' and yet there were several men smoking away unrestrained. How glad I was to get on board the cars!"

After they rode for about an hour and a half, the three of them reached Norwich. No one met them, so they had to walk nearly a mile dragging their baggage with them. Finally, at six o'clock in the morning, they reached the Greer's home where they were to stay, only to find the place all locked up. It was still dark, and no one was awake yet. They rang and rang the bell, but that did no good. They began pounding on doors and windows until someone heard them and let them in. Ellen had just turned sixty-three years old.

Now back to Salamanca, New York, and our story.

Ellen kept a diary or journal in a bound book of blank pages. She always carried this book to record happenings, appointments, and special things she wanted to remember. For the date of November 4, 1890, she left half the page empty, planning to fill in the details of the vision later. She eventually filled not only that half page with notes of her Salamanca vision, but she spilled over to other pages as well and filled them. Other visions on this subject followed, and a great deal of information was given to her. She wrote it all down. She was remembering that strange night of November 3 with clear insight. But this was all later; for the present she could not recall the details of the vision.

When she got back to Battle Creek, she began to prepare for the 1891 General Conference meetings to be held in March. Three times during that General Conference session she tried to tell the story of the Salamanca vision to a crowded audience in the tabernacle. All three times, her mind went blank. What was going on? Although distressed, she covered it up by saying she would have more to say about this vision later—and continued with her sermon.

Before we go further with the amazing story of the Salamanca vision, let's pause to look at the related visions she was given about this time and the information that she received. Much of what she was shown in these visions referred to the publishing houses—the Review and Herald and Pacific Press. Both were heavily involved in producing commercial work. "It reached the point at times when approximately 70 percent of the printing was commercial work and 30 percent denominational printing."[20] She was told in vision that this must stop.

She was also given information regarding authors. Both houses were trying to gain control of all literary products. This meant lower royalties for authors, while the income of the publishing houses was increasing. "It was argued that those in positions of management in the publishing house were in a better position to understand the needs of the cause, and know how to use profits which came from literature, than were the individual authors. The authors, they [publishing house managers] felt, might fall short in proper stewardship of royalty incomes. . . . This resulted in cutting off a fair royalty income to authors of the books published by the house."[21]

Working for personal gain in church institutions was another subject addressed in the visions. "He who is selfish and grasping, eager to take every dollar he can get from our institutions for his service, is binding about the work of God; verily he has his reward."[22]

"Men who are controlled by selfish desires should not remain connected with our institutions."[23]

Consolidation of the publishing houses, as well as of medical facilities such as sanitariums, was another issue dealt with by the visions. The counsel was that such consolidation should not take place. "During the year 1890, much thought had been given by leading men connected with the management of the Review and Herald Publishing Association, to a proposal for the consolidation of the work of the publishing houses under one board of control. The proposed union of the publishing interests was advocated as a means of securing unity, economy, and efficiency. At the same time the hope was expressed that at no distant day all the sanitariums might be brought under one ownership and control."[24]

To all of this, Ellen White was instructed to say No!

Now it's time to look at that special, elusive vision that took place in Salamanca, New York, on November 3, 1890. Why couldn't Ellen remember it when she tried? What was it all about? For answers, we turn to the General Conference Session of 1891.

Sabbath afternoon, March 7, 1891, Ellen White spoke on the special features of our faith and how vital it was for the church to preach the Word. She urged that in no way was the message to be covered up because of the false idea that minimizing certain aspects of truth "would avoid prejudice." Later in the day, after attending a ministers' meeting, General Conference President O. A. Olsen asked her if she would be present at the early meeting the next morning. She said that she would not be there because she was tired and needed to rest.

The next morning, several ministers, including her son Willie, were passing her house around 5:30 and saw that lights were on all over the house. Willie knew his mother had not planned to go to the meeting. Was she sick again? He and a friend raced up the stairs to her room to see what was going on.

They found Ellen out of bed, dressed, and writing. She turned as they entered and told them an angel had awakened her by shaking her arm at three o'clock. The angel told her to go to the morning meeting and tell the Salamanca vision. She had been writing for two hours.

When they arrived at the meeting, everyone was in prayer. Elder Olsen was surprised to see Ellen; he had been sure she would not be there. "We are glad to see you," he told Ellen. "Do you have a message for us this morning?"

"Indeed, I have!" came her strong reply.

With a bundle of papers under her arm, she walked to the front of the room and began to talk. She began by discussing the publishing work of the church and God's plan for it. Then she began telling the content of the vision that had eluded her memory for so long. It was clear in her mind now! She told how the angel had asked her to "follow me" as he led her into a room at the

Review and Herald office in Battle Creek. She saw a number of men in heated debate. They were discussing the editorial policy of the magazine *The American Sentinel.*

"I saw one of the men," she said, "take a copy of the *Sentinel,* hold it high over his head, and say, 'Unless these articles on the Sabbath and the Second Coming come out of the paper, we can no longer use it as an organ of the Religious Liberty Association.' " Ellen told about that meeting, describing the views and attitudes of the leading speakers. She heard harsh words spoken and saw wrong decisions being made. She spoke for an hour or more about the meeting she had seen in vision. Then she gave the advice the angel had given her for this group. This done, she sat down.

Elder Olsen, president of the General Conference, didn't know what to do or say. He was bewildered by what he had heard. He said he knew of no such meeting ever taking place. People in the audience were also puzzled; low whispers and murmurs began to be heard. No one seemed to know what to do next.

Then, amid all the confusion, a man began to rise slowly from his seat. And when he spoke, he did so in a voice that everyone in the room could hear. "I was in that meeting," he said. Then he added two electrifying words—"last night!"

Everyone was talking now. He continued speaking, and there was a hush again. "And I am the man who made the remarks about the articles in the paper, holding it high over my head. I am sorry to say that I am on the wrong side; but I take this opportunity to place myself on the right side."[25]

He sat down.

People were stunned. Ellen White herself was startled. She was the one who now seemed confused. In words clearly heard by those sitting close to her she said, "Last night!" She kept repeating those words over and over again in bewilderment—"Last night!" "Last night!" She was in shock. The vision had been given to her in Salamanca, New York, months before. Yet the meeting had actually occurred only last night! She couldn't believe it.

Another man stood in the audience. "I was in that meeting. Last night, after the close of the conference, some of us met in my room in the Review office, where we locked ourselves in, and there took up and discussed the questions and the matter that has been presented to us this morning." Then he added, "If I should have begun to give a description of what took place, and the personal attitude of those in the room, I could not have given it as exactly and correctly as it has been given by Sister White. I now see that I was in error; that the position that I took was not correct; and from the light that has been given this morning, I acknowledge that I was wrong."[26]

Others who had been in that locked room the night before stood to their feet and bore the same testimony, saying that Ellen White had accurately described the meeting and the attitude of those in attendance.

Before the devotional closed that Sunday morning, the Religious Liberty Association group were called together. "They rescinded the action they had taken only five hours before."[27]

Later, Elder Olsen recalled, "Personally, I sat there in blank bewilderment. I did not know what she referred to. I had neither heard nor had any knowledge of the things that she presented, nor of such a meeting as she described. Indeed, I was so surprised, and the things she presented as having taken place in that meeting seemed so unreasonable. . . . Sister White had had no opportunity to have any knowledge of what had gone on in that room during the night in the Review office. . . . The Lord had shown it to her before the thing took place; and now, the very morning in which it took place, she had been, in a special manner, called by the Lord to present what had been shown her."[28]

"A. T. Robinson related that those who attended that morning meeting had no breakfast that day. The meeting which began at five-thirty and usually closed at six-thirty, continued until well on in the forenoon. . . . Men of strong iron wills, who the night before manifested a spirit of unyielding stubbornness, confessed with tears and brokenness of voice. . . . There came a spirit of unity and sweet communion. The *Sentinel*, now called *Liberty*, has continued to this day to bear a mighty message of truth to the people."[29]

On several occasions, Ellen White had tried to relate the events of the vision she had received on November 3, 1890, but without success. Now it became clear just why the Lord had prevented her from relating the Salamanca vision earlier. He reserved the contents of that vision until the right moment for them to be told. He foresaw a church crisis looming on the horizon and then led the situation to a powerful climax, thus averting a serious mistake. He also demonstrated in a dramatic, effective way unquestioned evidence about the reality, dependability, and integrity of the Spirit of Prophecy.

1. Arthur White, *Ellen G. White: The Lonely Years*, 3:453.
2. Ibid., 455.
3. *Testimonies to Ministers and Gospel Workers*, xxv.
4. Arthur White, *Ellen G. White: The Lonely Years,* 3:460.
5. Ibid., 458.
6. Ibid.
7. Ibid.
8. Ibid., 461.
9. Ibid., 456.
10. Ibid.
11. *Testimonies to Ministers and Gospel Workers*, xxiv.
12. *Sermons and Talks by Ellen G. White* (Silver Spring, Md.: Ellen G. White Estate, 1990), 1:143-149.
13. Arthur White, *Ellen G. White: The Lonely Years,* 3:462.
14. Ibid., 464, 465.
15. Ibid., 465.
16. Ibid., 466.
17. Ibid., 467.
18. *Life Sketches of Ellen G. White*, 316.
19. *The Spirit of Prophecy Treasure Chest*, 42.

20. Ibid.
21. *Testimonies to Ministers and Gospel Workers,* xxxvii.
22. Ibid., xxix.
23. *Selected Messages,* 2:195.
24. Ibid., 194.
25. *Life Sketches of Ellen G. White,* 311.
26. *The Spirit of Prophecy Treasure Chest,* 43.
27. Arthur White, *Ellen G. White: The Lonely Years,* 3:480, 481.
28. *The Spirit of Prophecy Treasure Chest,* 43, 44.
29. Arthur White, *Ellen G. White: The Lonely Years,* 3:481.
30. Ibid., 482.

CHAPTER TWO

Down Under

*I*n 1893 Ellen had passed her sixty-fifth birthday. Today, this is the age when most people think of retirement. But to stop her work for age, sickness, hardship, or anything else was the furthest thing from Ellen's mind. She would work until her life ended. That is just the way she was.

She commented on this in the *Review and Herald* of June 13, 1893: "Sometimes when I feel unable to fill my appointments, I say, In faith I will place myself in position. I will go to the meeting, and stand upon my feet, although feeling unable to say a word; and whenever I have done this, I have had strength given me to rise above all infirmities and to bear the message the Lord has given me for the people."[1]

Did you notice her use of the word *bear*? She knew well what that word meant. Her work was never easy even when she was well. In that same article she also wrote: "We have traveled about twenty-five hundred miles by sea and by land, and I have written over three hundred pages of letter paper. I have spoken to the people forty-one times."[2] All this was accomplished in a three-month period. Remember, too, that travel a hundred or more years ago was not like travel today. Did you notice her reference to writing three hundred pages? Hold that thought a moment as we look at another issue of the *Review and Herald*, dated December 5, 1893.

"We have now been in this missionary field [New Zealand and Australia] nearly two years. For eleven months of this time, because of sickness, I was unable to labor in public. At times, with much inconvenience and suffering, I spoke in the church at Melbourne; but although I could not labor in a public manner during these months of suffering, I was enabled to write 2400 pages of letter paper upon themes that were essential to the progress of the work."[3]

So we find her writing again, and this time, it's 2,400 pages of that "eternal writing," as her husband James had called it.

Ellen was in pain much of the time she was "down under" in Australia and New Zealand. But in spite of her pain, she never thought seriously of quitting or going back home. Her travel experiences in Australia alone would be enough to fill several books. There were rare occasions, however (and they really were rare), when she became so depressed that she considered retirement. "I have seasons of temptation, when infirmities press so heavily upon me, and at such times I ask myself, 'Am I really in the way of my duty? Is it not time I retired from active labor?' "

"Then when I stand before the people after such a battle with the enemy, the Holy Spirit comes to me as a divine helper. I have the assurance that my work is not to close yet."[4] There we have the human element; Ellen White had to deal with discouragement just like the rest of us.

It isn't the purpose of this book to try to tell everything that happened to Ellen White "down under." Instead, the focus will be on what may be called "adventures"—mainly events happening in New Zealand.

These "adventures" will provide an insight into what this little woman was made of, her driving spirit, and, of course, her great stamina. They will also tell of the effect of her work upon the people around her. For it made no difference to Mrs. White whether or not she knew a person; she still attempted to have a decided effect on that person for good. For instance, she had a habit of carrying a number of church magazines or books with her whenever she traveled. And she put them to good use!

Picture her on the south island of New Zealand. The year was 1893. It was three o'clock in the morning, and she was wide awake. She was going on a train ride and was all excited about it. She couldn't sleep. For Ellen, the thrill of seeing a new and different place was almost like the excitement of a child with a new toy.

Packing had kept her up most of the night. She finally woke Emily Campbell, one of her workers, at five o'clock, and the two of them finished closing up trunks and suitcases, rolled up bedding, and then waited for the luggage wagon. Their "taxi" came at six o'clock. It was a small covered buggy pulled by a sleepy horse!

The station was only a mile and a half away, but it was slow going. Yet there Ellen and her party were, ready even ahead of time, when the train arrived at 6:30. Four people made the trip: Ellen, her son Willie, Emily Campbell, and a man whose name we no longer know.

They traveled second class, and the ride was far from comfortable. Passengers sat on hard wooden benches facing each other, with an aisle between. This reminded Ellen of the horse-drawn streetcars in American cities. They were almost the only passengers at first because it was so early. There wasn't much for them to do except to look at the scenery. They counted thirteen tunnels as the little train puffed its way among giant fern forests in the mountains.

Tiny stations appeared from time to time, and the train stopped at all of them. As usual, Ellen sat spellbound with what she saw.

She had never seen country like this. Fellow passengers, she observed, usually rode short distances. Many were tall, muscular, and dark skinned. She was told these were the Maori people—original, or native, New Zealanders thought to be of Polynesian origin.

As hour after hour passed, Ellen kept her eyes on a quiet, well-dressed man. He was extremely polite. Her curiosity finally got the best of her. She whispered to Willie, "Go over and talk with that man and find out if he knows English."

To her joy, the man not only knew English but had gone to a mission school for several years. His father was a Maori chief.

That's all Ellen needed to know. She smiled and began a conversation. In time, she handed him some of the church papers she had with her. Still polite, the man thanked her graciously.

When their conversation ended, the man began reading the papers she had given him. But Ellen kept looking at him from the corner of her eyes. She was overjoyed when she saw that he had become so involved with what he was reading that he almost missed his station stop when it was called. As her trip continued, there was a smile on her face, and a few less magazines for her to carry.[5]

New Zealand is an island nation. North Island and South Island are the two main land masses. There are a number of other islands belonging to the country, some of which are still uninhabited—such as Three Kings, Snares, and Bounty. Not counting these minor islands, the land mass of New Zealand is 103,736 square miles. No place, on either of the two large islands, is more than eighty miles from the coast. Mountains and hills can be seen from any point of land. Almost in the center of North Island is Burning Mountain rising to about six thousand feet. Burning Mountain is actually a volcano with constant action and occasional eruptions. Its real name is Tongariro. Nearby, in the area known as the Lake District, are hot lakes, boiling springs, and hissing geysers. Earthquakes are common here.[6]

New Zealand is a British Commonwealth with a constitutional monarchy. Australia, its closest neighbor of any size, is 1,200 miles to the northwest. The islands making up New Zealand were first discovered by Europeans in 1642 when Abel Janszoon Tasman, a Dutchman, sighted the west coast of South Island. After landing, however, he was run off by the Maoris. He next sailed north but did not attempt a second landing anywhere. Captain James Cook, an Englishman, did manage to land in 1769. He experienced very little trouble with the Maoris. In fact, they seemed to like this Pakeha (the Maori word for a white person). Cook sailed his ships around both islands and made at least four more trips to this area during his lifetime.

Others Europeans followed, including French, Spanish, and English explorers. The English established whaling stations. These soon became wild and lawless due to the influence of seamen who deserted their ships and an influx of escaped convicts from Australia.

Missionaries from Sydney, Australia, arrived in New Zealand in 1814, led by Samuel Marsden. Others soon came from Europe.

About this time, the Maoris obtained gunpowder and muskets and soon became involved in bloody intertribal wars. Battles with the white man became numerous as well, usually over the details of a land deal that had gone sour. In 1833, a party was sent from New South Wales to restore order but was unable to do so. But when Captain William Hobson, of the British navy, arrived, things began to change. Hobson proclaimed British sovereignty over New Zealand on January 30, 1840. The treaty of Waitangi was made on February 6. This treaty granted Maori chiefs and tribes undisturbed possession of their lands.

More and more English settlers began to arrive in New Zealand, and the next few years were rather peaceful—until Hobson's death in 1843. Then disputes between the English settlers and the Maori tribes began to break out again. In 1852, Sir

George Grey (at that time mere "Captain" Grey) came and formed settlements with a representative form of government. A constitution was created providing for a legislature, the membership of which would come from all parts of New Zealand. Even so, jealousies and conflicts arose again—this time because of the role of the central authority. Finally, to satisfy everyone, a provincial government was established in 1876. Local government was entrusted to counties and cities.

But there was still no peace, and war broke out again. Hostilities began on North Island between the Maori and white settlers. Once more, land was the main issue. The British sent troops, who eventually saw action in three battles between 1860 and 1870. The Maori fought bravely, but their's was a hopeless situation. The war continued, but the white settlers, too, were having a difficult time of it. The war debt was huge. Both sides wanted the conflict to end, but neither knew how to stop fighting without losing face. In the end a compromise was reached. The Maori's courage and loyalty to their code won a grudging respect from the white settlers, and the compromise ensured the Maori's positions in parliament and schools for their children. And their land rights were to be respected.[7]

The Maori people are a proud, handsome race of Polynesians; they make up about 9 percent of New Zealand's population. Most are tall with broad faces, brown eyes, and black wavy hair. The original Maoris lived in remote villages and made their living by fishing and hunting. Later, some turned to farming. They were skilled in woodcarving, decorating war canoes and communal houses with delicate designs.

As cities grew in New Zealand, they attracted many of the Maori people to them. In time, Maoris filled government positions, entered industry, and were found in almost all professional fields. But in spite of their assimilation into the white culture, the Maori have never forgotten their past and its customs. They conduct large gatherings known as *hui* for weddings, funerals, and the opening of buildings. Although they speak English, their own language is generally used at these gatherings. Many of the Maori people can trace their Christian beliefs to the late 1800s and a strong missionary movement on the islands.[8]

What long-distance travel there was in New Zealand during the late 1800s was made by train. But most of the population, both Maori and White, traveled locally by horse-drawn vehicles, on horseback, or by foot.

Returning again to Ellen White and her train travel, we find that she usually chose to go second class. The reason was simple: it was cheaper. On one train trip from Napier to Palmerston April 9, 1893, Ellen was suffering greatly from a hip problem, but as she boarded the train, she said, "We [Emily Campbell and Willie were with her on this trip] could make a comfortable seat with cushions, and I think I did not suffer any more in the second class than I should in the first, and we would have to pay one pound, one shilling extra for us three if we rode in first class."[9] When it came to her own comfort, Ellen sacrificed. Yet if a real financial need arose, she gave liberally.

There was also a second reason for traveling second class: She could study and communicate directly with the ordinary people of the country, as she did with the Maori chief's son.

The little trains of her day were not long in length. This was especially true on North Island because of the number of steep grades and "S" type curves. Most of these railroads were (and still are) single track. This further limits trains to run at full capacity. These short trains were also another reason why there was so much crowding at times. To this day there are trains in New Zealand that attach passenger "wagons" to freight services. One such train is called the "Cabbage Train," which runs from Picton to Christchurch on South Island.[10]

August 19, 1893, found Ellen on yet another train. She and

her party climbed aboard a train headed for the city of Hastings. There was only one second-class passenger coach. The car was almost full, and Ellen's group had trouble finding seats together. But once seated and the luggage put away, they began to look at their fellow passengers. Most were Maoris. That was no problem, but what Ellen saw and heard was. For many of the Maoris were drunk. "Many were so drunk," she said, "they hardly knew what they were doing."[11]

There were also a few European passengers in the car, and this was the source of the trouble, for they were the ones who had sold the alcohol to the Maoris. Ellen became a little nervous, especially with the yelling, stomping of feet, and heavy smoking all around her. She knew what was in store, and in fact, it had already started—she felt one of her severe headaches beginning.

What did she do? She did what she always did. She bowed her head and prayed for help. The answer was instantaneous. Sitting across the aisle from her sat three young Maori men. They, too, were watching the drunken mess. They seemed to be greatly embarrassed that some of their countrymen would act like that. Ellen took a good hard look at these three. As she did so, she noticed how different they acted from the others. They had a look of disgust on their faces.

Then quite suddenly, and to the surprise of everyone in the car, there was music. Voices were singing Christian hymns. Those three young men were singing hymn after hymn, one after another! Ellen could hardly believe her ears. She was so startled and relieved that when there was a pause in the singing, she spoke up and thanked the men for what they were doing. Smiling, they pointed to the drunken Maoris and said, "They are showing their colors, and we must show our colors."[12]

The train pulled into Hastings around eight o'clock in the evening. Before Ellen could get off the train, the three young men jumped up, helped her and her friends down the steps, and then got their luggage for them.

"We could only thank them," Ellen said.[13] She learned later that the three were students and had another twenty miles to travel, on foot, before they reached their school. She was greatly impressed. Ellen liked the Maori people and had strong feelings for them. Now, having seen these three young men and their thoughtfulness, she liked them even more.

Young people were one of Ellen's first priorities. She would do everything she could to help a young person in need. While talking with a sixteen-year-old Maori boy one day, she learned he was making an effort to attend the Adventist school in Melbourne, Australia. But it was hopeless. There was no money. That is all she needed to hear. Ellen and her son Willie personally paid for the boy's transportation to Australia and his tuition.

But there is more to the story. When the ship was almost ready to sail for Australia, the boy learned of a death in his home village. Since he was the chief's son, he had to return. He was also told that he must take part in the funeral. This meant taking an active part in drinking, dancing, wailing, and other ceremonies. The boy went home anyway.

But when he arrived he found that the entire village was in an uproar. People were shouting and arguing and taking sides. The source of the trouble was this young man. The villagers knew he was a Christian and some did not feel he should be allowed to take part in the funeral. Others felt he should. As tempers grew to a rage, the young man feared that a riot or bloodshed would break out. Then as the tempo increased, he saw a chance to escape. Quietly and unnoticed, he melted into the darkness and slipped away. Racing for the railroad station, he caught a train for Napier and was soon once more on his way to Australia and school.

Ellen helped other young men who accepted Seventh-day Adventist beliefs, many of whom became baptized members. And back in their home villages, heathen priests and even a few local church leaders were furious.

Ellen had a young friend she called Pomeroy. His native name was Maui Pomare. This fellow was also a chief's son—"a chief of high repute," Ellen reported.[14] When he went to America for training to become a medical missionary, Ellen paid the bills for Pomeroy to Battle Creek College in the United States, including his travel expenses all the way by ship and rail.

Ellen did the same without hesitation for several other young people. She wanted them to have a Christian education. She wrote: "Oh, how deeply interested I am, that these young men shall become prepared to do the missionary work so essential to be done in their own nation [New Zealand]."[15]

The gospel story was first heard by the Maoris of New Zealand in 1814 when Samuel Marsden, from New South Wales, began to work among them. This was true pioneer missionary work; the Maori people were savages and even cannibals at that time. And they had great hatred for the white man. But through faith, hard work, and a great deal of prayer Marsden found a few converts. It was a tiny beginning, but it was a breakthrough.

Seventy-one years later, in 1885, the voice of S. N. Haskell was heard bringing the third angel's message to New Zealand. He started his work in the city of Auckland, on North Island. Two of his very first converts were Mr. and Mrs. Edward Hare. Edward had been preparing to take the gospel to the Maoris when he joined the Adventist Church. Edward was so excited at what he had learned that he convinced Haskell to visit his father, Joseph Hare, and the rest of the family. The Hare family lived 160 miles north of Auckland in a place named Kaeo. This was close to Maori country in the most northern section of North Island. Edward Hare was convinced his family must hear the message he had heard and accepted.

Joseph Hare was a Methodist minister. He had been married twice and had a lot of mouths to feed. Counting his children and stepchildren, the number came to twenty-four. Father Hare, as he was called, had been a schoolteacher for twenty-four years in Ireland before moving to New Zealand. The second Mrs. Hare was called "doctor" because of her work with Maori women and children.

Haskell preached from Father Hare's pulpit for three Sundays. That was all it took for Father Hare to join Edward, along with a few others, in accepting the Adventist message.

Robert Hare, another of Joseph's sons, was also a local minister. He accepted the Adventist teachings, and one month after his baptism, he sailed for the United States and the Adventist college at Healdsburg, California. He wanted a Christian education because he was determined to preach his new-found faith.

Edward, meanwhile, still had a burning desire to take the gospel to the Maori people. A few of the natives were Sunday keepers, but he wanted them to know about the Seventh-day Sabbath and its message. "We must print a paper for them," he said, "but how?" The Maori alphabet has only twelve letters (a, e, i, o, u, h, k, m, n, p, r, t) and the 'ng' sound.

Father Hare just smiled. "Never mind that," he said. And the rest of the family smiled too. They knew he had a plan. Working with the right people, he eventually solved the problem, and a Maori paper was published.

Edward began to make his living by selling some of Ellen White's books—especially *The Great Controversy*. Many of those books went on board ships that sailed all over the Pacific. In the meantime, Edward's wife began writing letters to other islands about their new-found faith. Soon the message began to spread.

Years later, when Ellen White visited New Zealand, she was urged to go see the Hare family at Kaeo. She did. And she even wrote about it. "Here is a company of interesting people," she said, "a father, and his children and grandchildren. Father Hare is now in his seventies. . . . He is a man much respected. The community was so anxious to see us that we consented to take this trip from Auckland to Kaeo.

"They have a little chapel which was built by the Hare family. . . .We feel pleased that we can visit this church consisting mostly of the members of this one family."[16]

To make the trip, Ellen had to ride on a coastal boat named *The Clansman*. This ship made the trip from Auckland to Kaeo once a week and took twenty-four hours! Ellen didn't like her cabin on the boat and decided not to use it. "It was close," she said, meaning it was crowded and stuffy, "and the berths in staterooms [were] narrow and hard as a board." At this time, she was having so much hip trouble again that it was hard for her to walk.

The crew of the ship was trying to be nice to her, but the journey was difficult. She sat, wrapped like a mummy, on the deck in a chair that she had brought along. She also brought her own bed on board. The smoking room was cleared for her comfort, but wouldn't you know it, her bed wouldn't go through the door! Now what was she going to do? Besides hurting more and more from the pain in her hip, she had no place to go.

Willie and the steward took over. They went looking for another place to put the bed and found a spot on the other side of the ship. They hung up rugs as a shield from the wind. Then they set the bed behind the rugs and put Ellen in it. Her comment was that she was "oh so grateful for the privilege." Emily and Willie slept beside her in steamer chairs, one on each side. They didn't want her to fall out of bed and roll across the deck, and maybe into the ocean!

When the ship arrived at Whangarei Harbor, Father Joseph Hare and his son Metcalf were there to meet them. All of them got into a small boat, called a skiff, and rowed another three miles with all those travelers and their luggage. There was no mention of Ellen's bed or chair. Let's not even think about those! It took two hours to row that little boat the three miles. Can you picture it? "Willie sat at the end of the boat at the helm, his back to my back," wrote Ellen, "to give me support and to guide the boat." The two Hare men "stood up in the boat, each with an oar, and were guided by word and motion of head." And so it went. Too bad there weren't any pictures taken!

They stayed the rest of that night in a house near the boat landing. When morning came, so did Father Hare—with his carriage. He drove them another three miles to his home at the foot of a mountain.

This was the most pleasant part of the trip for Ellen. She was excited by what she saw. Tree ferns were everywhere, and mountains ran like links in a chain, one after another. She was spellbound by the beauty. Father Hare's home was at the base of a wooded mountain. There was a sparkling stream, orchards of apples, pears, peaches, plum, and quince. Beyond this were pine trees.

Ellen planned on two weeks for the trip to Kaeo. But bad weather set in, and the time stretched to three weeks.

For Ellen White, one of the high points of this trip was a visit to Maori country. With the Hares as her guide, she was allowed to attend one of the tribal councils. "We saw large preparations made," she wrote. "Tents [were] pitched in a beautiful location, where the house of the priest of the Maoris was located. There were beautiful tall evergreen trees bordering the enclosure and here were collected a large congregation of the Maoris for a council meeting. It was quite a sight. Looked like a camp meeting. The tents were very low, yet manifested considerable skill and taste in their formation. The dresses of many were gaudy, as if to out-rival the rainbow."

The council considered Ellen to be an honored guest and asked her to speak. She was delighted and chose for her topic the soon coming of the Lord. Her native audience was pleased and then excited and happy to hear what she said. They were also quite vocal about it and wanted Jesus to come now and take them to

Himself. "Oh," said many of them, "that I could live to see Him."

The time passed too quickly, and as Ellen was about to leave, she shared one of the family's happiest moments. Two of Father Hare's daughters were baptized—Minnie, twenty, and Susan, fourteen—and no one could be happier than old Father Hare.

Ellen's trip to the top of North Island was now over. One can almost imagine her all wrapped up like a mummy as she sailed back down the coast to Auckland. With eyes closed, doubtless she was living and listening once again to the joyful sights and sounds of the Maori people she had grown to love. I'm sure she never forgot their words: "Oh, that I could live to see Him." We can almost see her smile. She was so happy.

1. *Review and Herald*, June 13, 1893. Ellen White wrote this article while in Palmerston, New Zealand.

2. Ibid.

3. *Review and Herald*, December 5, 1893.

4. Arthur L. White, *Ellen G. White: The Australian Years, 1891-1900*, 4:71, 72.

5. This experience is based on information found in materials produced by the E. G. White Estate for Spirit of Prophecy Emphasis Week for Seventh-day Adventist Schools, September 1974, 40, 41.

6. Ibid., 33.

7. *Encyclopedia Americana*, International edition, 279.

8. *World Book Encyclopedia*, 1987, 13:135.\

9. Arthur L. White, *Ellen G. White: The Australian Years, 1891-1900*, 4:89.

10. R. J. Johnston, *The New Zealanders: How They Live and Work*.

11. Based on information found in materials produced by the E. G. White Estate for Spirit of Prophecy Emphasis Week for Seventh-day Adventist Schools, September 1974, 35.

12. Ibid., 36.

13. Ibid.

14. Ibid., 37.

15. Ibid.

16. The story of Ellen White's visit to the Hare family is based on information found in materials produced by the E. G. White Estate for Spirit of Prophecy Emphasis Week for Seventh-day Adventist Schools, September 1974.

CHAPTER THREE

A Minivacation— I

West of the city of Wellington, on New Zealand's North Island, runs a rugged shoreline that stretches northward for miles along the Tasman Sea. Sharp twists and turns, carved by centuries of wild storms, create rough cliffs of unusual beauty.

In 1893 a narrow ribbon of unpaved road followed close beside this wild coastline. It was a hazardous road to travel. The challenge of deep ruts and rocks made traveling a real hardship, but it was a road. And for those few who chose to live along this rocky beach road it was a way of life.

Late one July afternoon a tiny object could be seen moving in the distance. It was a small horse pulling a two-wheeled trap (a small cart or a light carriage). Progress was slow as it bumped and jolted its passengers along the coastal road. Sometimes the trap was lost to view as it rounded a bend or was hidden by an outcropping of rock. But then it would reappear again in the open stretches.

A small side road appeared, and the trap swerved to follow it. Finally, it stopped before a simple building, a schoolhouse. Two children rushed from the building to the waiting trap and jumped aboard, crowding the passengers even more. The buggy was extremely overloaded but no one cared, for all was laughter and fun as the little horse headed for the main road going south.

The sparkling sea off to the right moved and shimmered in the sun. From time to time great silver sprays of water splashed high into the air, casting rainbows among the rocks. But the little trap went on and on. It never stopped.

As the horse turned at last into a small lane leading to a hilltop house, one passenger, at least, was quite worn out—Ellen White. That ride along the beach had completed a round trip of fifteen rough miles. The house looked wonderful to her as she stepped to the ground. Flowers, bushes, and beautiful trees greeted her. Mountains and hills rose in the distance, and a view overlooked the sweeping curve of the bay. Ellen loved it all.

Later that night she wrote this in her diary: "Although the two-wheeled trap was not as easy as a phaeton [carriage], yet I enjoyed the ride, jolting and all, for I can only walk a little ways on account of my hip." Then she went on to add, "I shall take all the rides I can in this trap and know it will do me good. The scenery is very nice and we had sunshine all the way."[1]

The two children who had joined the trap at the schoolhouse lived in the hilltop house where Ellen and her friend Emily Campbell were guests. Their mother, Martha Brown, had invited Ellen and Emily to her home for a week-long vacation. The place was called Long Point and was situated a mile from the railroad station at Paremata. Ellen had met Martha Brown in Wellington. Martha was a cook in the city, and the two had become friends.

The week at the Brown home was to be Ellen's minivacation. She had gone there to get away from her heavy workload in the city; she needed a rest.

Let's look at a few of the reasons why Ellen was so worn out. And as we do, one wonders how she was able to get through it all! There were so many problems demanding her attention. Here are a few.

In August she made this diary entry. "For more than a year I was unable to bend the knees to kneel down." Yet, she continued, "I see so much to be thankful for." Then she said the Lord had been her restorer because "I am able to kneel down now."[2]

Ellen had severe hip problems. Besides that, she was also in pain because of her teeth. She had only eight left, and of these eight, some were abscessed. She had met an Adventist dentist—a lady by the name of Dr. Caro—in April while attending a camp meeting in Napier. So she wrote to Dr. Caro. It was time to do something about those teeth.

Dr. Caro's husband was a medical doctor. He was not an Adventist, but he was friendly to his wife's beliefs. Mrs. Caro carried forward many missionary activities among the Maoris. There was no objection from her husband when she paid the bills to send young Maoris off to Adventist schools in the United States.

So Ellen set the date of July 5 for Mrs. Caro to come to Wellington and pull out all her teeth.

In a letter to Willie she wrote, "Sister Caro is here. . . .You know what will take place. I am not afraid. My teeth are troubling me a little too much for comfort."[3]

At breakfast on the morning of the fifth, the Dr. asked Ellen, "Are you sorry to see me?"

"I am pleased to meet [see] Sister Caro, certainly," Ellen replied. "Not so certain whether to meet Mrs. Dr. Caro, dentist."

"At ten o'clock [a.m.]" Ellen wrote in her diary, "I am in the chair, and in a short time eight teeth were drawn. I was glad the job was over. I did not wince or groan."[4]

But the story is not over. Once the teeth were out, Ellen saw that there was something wrong with the dentist. She was trembling like a leaf. Her hands shook, and she was in pain. Several things made the doctor fall apart. First, she had been sick on the train ride to Wellington. Second, she didn't want to hurt Ellen, and the thoughts of pulling all those teeth was also getting to her. She knew Ellen to be allergic to almost everything that would deaden pain. As a result, Ellen had taken nothing to prevent pain during the extraction.

So with Ellen's ordeal now over, the dentist was in trouble! Wouldn't you know it! It was Ellen herself, of all people, who took charge and helped the dentist to an easy chair and found something to bring relief to her!

With no teeth for at least two months, Ellen knew she could never keep her speaking appointments. But that didn't stop her from doing things. She simply changed course and went back to her writing until her new teeth arrived.

Teeth were not all that was causing Ellen trouble. A telegram arrived saying there was trouble aboard the ship Pitcairn. (The Pitcairn was an Adventist mission ship funded—at least in part— with Sabbath School offerings for that purpose.) Since it was due to arrive in the port of Auckland soon, she decided that Willie should go to the ship to see if he could help solve the situation. Then he was to stay with the ship until it reached Wellington. Willie met the ship at Gisborne. One week later there was no word from the ship or Willie, and Ellen was worried.

Then, to her relief, word came on November 11, while she was being fitted for her new teeth at Dr. Caro's home. The ship was safe and on its way to Wellington. There had been bad weather.

Next came a telegram announcing the arrival from Africa of O. A. Olsen, president of the General Conference. He would be in Wellington for the camp meeting there. And, of course, he expected Ellen to be present.

What else could happen to her now?

Well, something did. She received a letter from her son Edson that shook her more than all the other problems she was going through. It crushed her. Edson was living in Chicago and owned a printing business that was heavily in debt. A church worker before the move to Chicago, he now stated flatly in this letter to his mother, "I am not at all religiously inclined."[5] Stunned by this news and still hurt with shock, she responded. This is what she wrote:

"Why should you express yourself as you have done?" (Ellen didn't baby Edson!) She continued. "Why use such firm language? Why do you have any satisfaction in this selfish independence? If you were a man unacquainted with truth, I could address you in a different way, approach you by presenting the truth in all its beauty and attractive loveliness. But this would not move you. The answer would be, 'I knew all that before. I am not as ignorant as you suppose.' "[6]

Exhausted, she decided to finish the letter the next day (July 21). She went to bed with the heavy heart of a mother. Then quite suddenly, at 1:30 in the morning, she was wide awake. As she described it, she was "full of terror."

She had been dreaming, and it scared her. She had seen Edson in her dream. He was toying with powerful waves at a beach. He had friends with him, and they were all doing the same. But he was the leader. He had laughed at warnings of a powerful undertow. Ellen called to her son in the dream, trying to warn him. But he couldn't hear her. She was told in her dream that Edson could see her but not hear her. She was also told that if she would motion him away by her actions, he would obey. She tried. But he laughed at her concern and went closer to the water's danger point.

Suddenly she saw a strong swimmer tie himself to shore with a rope in an effort to save him. Edson laughed again and was instantly in the undertow. The harder he fought, the more he was dragged under. At that instant, Ellen woke up with a terrible scream lingering in her ears. It had come from Edson in her dream.

Trying to compose herself, she slowly got out of bed and went to the half-written letter she had started the day before. She was shaken. She began to write, telling her son all she had seen in the dream. Her words were direct and strong. "The undertow," she wrote, "what does it represent? It represents Satan and a set, independent, stubborn will of your own which has reached even against God."[7]

She continued writing to her son in the middle of the night. "You are no more a child. I would that you were. I would cradle you in my arms, watch over you as I have done. But you are a man grown. You have taken the molding of your character out of the hands of your mother, out of the hands of God. And are placing defective, rotten timbers in the building." She went on. "And you . . . coolly state you will not change your course, that is, as I understand it, come into submission to God, until your debts are paid and you have a reliable competency [livelihood]. . . . You have been strong one hour, vacillating the next. I am now determined to press upon your notice and make you hear: 'This is the undertow.' "

She stopped writing. Tears were rolling down her face and splashing to the floor. This was her boy she was writing! Finally she managed to pull herself together. Wiping her eyes, she closed the letter with these words: "I cannot save you; God alone can save you. But work, while Jesus invites you."

She signed her letter "In harmony with God, Mother."[8]

The letter was mailed and made its way across the ocean. When Edson opened it and began to read, he seemed to see his mother calling to him, beckoning to him, above the thunder of the waves. On August 10, 1893, he wrote these words in reply to his mother: "I have surrendered fully and completely, and never enjoyed life before as I am now. . . . I have no desire for the amusements and pleasures that made up the sum of my enjoyments before. . . . I have left it all with my Saviour, and the burden does not bear me down any longer."[9]

Ellen wasted no time in answering his thrilling letter. She was thousands of miles away and had felt so helpless—until now. With joy in her heart, she wrote: "Never fail or be discouraged. It is that which you ought to have done long ago, and your mother will give you encouragement and her prayers and so will your brother. Years that have passed into eternity are beyond your power to recall, but through the grace of Christ you may labor in the vineyard for the Master."[10]

Ellen was beside herself with joy, thrilled through and through with Edson's decision. And her joy increased as she watched his steady progress in the years that followed. She thanked God every day for what He had done for her boy. She gave Him all the credit and glory.

And as for Edson, he went on to pioneer God's message. He worked among the Black people in the war-ravaged South following the terrible American Civil War. Ellen's son had come back, and he was back to stay!

---

1. Based on information found in materials produced by the E. G. White Estate for Spirit of Prophecy Emphasis Week for Seventh-day Adventist Schools, September 1974, 17.
2. Arthur L. White, *Ellen G. White: The Australian Years, 1891-1900,* 4:105.
3. Ibid., 98.
4. Ibid.
5. Ibid., 94.
6. Ibid.
7. Ibid., 96.
8. Ibid., 94-97.
9. Ibid., 97.
10. Ibid., 107.

A Minivacation— II

A s far as Ellen White was concerned, *vacation* was a strange word, belonging to another world. She never made time for such things. But somehow the invitation to spend some time at Long Point, the Brown's home near Paremata, had great appeal to her. She felt tired and stressed from everything that happened in the past few months. So she decided she would accept Mrs. Brown's invitation.

"One cannot keep upon one strain continuously without breaking down," she wrote. "It has been one steady strain early and late, but there must come a halt."[1]

So she snapped up Martha Brown's invitation and thought that friends, the sea air, and rest would be good for her. Her friend, Emily Campbell, went with her; Emily was in about the same condition as Ellen and needed a change also.

In the previous chapter we learned that Ellen had begun to relax and unwind while on those delightful yet bumpy and uncomfortable rides in the trap. As the days flew by, she began to feel her tensions fading away.

But to get a full picture of her little pleasure trip (and, for Ellen, that is just what it was), we must return to the beginning of her minivacation. And as we do so, we will discover that God had a hand in it as well. He was leading Ellen to Long Point for a definite reason.

Let's begin as Ellen boarded the train in Wellington. She was carrying a notebook and something to write with, because even on a trip like this, Ellen continued her writing. The ride was not long, maybe an hour or an hour and a half, that's all. Yet as she traveled, she wrote: "We passed through eight tunnels. The scenery was odd and romantic. Much of the road on this line is through a gorge, very deep in many places. Then we would see nice little farms in the valleys, and then again steep mountains and waterfalls."[2]

When she arrived at the Brown's home, she learned that the family consisted of Martha, in her late twenties, Martha's mother, a widow of eight years, and several brothers and sisters. Martha was one of thirteen children; she and her mother were the only Seventh-day Adventists in the family. A few of the thirteen children were married and had moved away.

The two youngest Brown children went to school every morning. Sometimes they walked the three miles. At other times they rode in the little trap, as they had done that day with Ellen as we saw in the last chapter. Ellen loved these little rides along the beach. She enjoyed not only the fresh sea air but the wonderful rugged scenery that went with it. This was just what she needed! By Wednesday she was feeling her old self again and became restless. She thought of all the work waiting for her in the city. So, with this strong urge to return, she began to pack. She wanted to be off to Wellington before the next Sabbath; she would leave the next morning, on Thursday.

But God had other plans, and things—strange things—

began to happen.

Ellen went to bed early Wednesday night. Her hip was better but still hurt. The train ride the next day would be hard on it. She needed rest, a solid good night's rest.

Thursday, August 3, Ellen made a determined effort to leave for the railway station. But it never happened. A violent storm broke over the coast. Heavy rain and strong winds whipped the storm as it became more intense. No one could go anywhere. So Ellen stayed one more day.

She went to bed early on Thursday night and slept well until about 4:00 a.m. Then she woke up suddenly and looked around in somewhat of a daze. She was confused. Where was she? She didn't know.

It was then that she saw an angel and knew she was in vision. But where was she? She wasn't in the Brown's home. She was in a dark, rough-looking building. It was dingy, dirty, and the lighting was bad. She looked at the angel with questions in her eyes. What was going on?

The angel understood and said, "Follow me." She did.

Together they entered a dimly lighted room. Once inside, she noticed people huddled around a table. They were all young people, some in their teens. But what were they doing? She looked closer. Young men were deeply absorbed in a game of cards, while the girls leaned forward watching. Vulgar language and comments were made. Obscene words were said, which the speakers would be ashamed of if they had known an angel and Ellen White were watching.

Ellen was puzzled. "Who are these young people?" she asked. And to herself she questioned why she was there to see this.

"Wait!" came the answer. Then suddenly the angel took her to another place. She was more confused than ever.

In the second place she saw the same young people again. But this time they were drinking beer and hard liquor. The alcohol had already taken effect, and there was loud laughing, boasting, jests, and showing off. The language was filthy.

Ellen was impatient now. She wanted answers. Why was she there? Who were these teenagers?

But when the answer came, she was not ready for it. Her reaction was complete shock. The angel said, "These young people are a portion of the family you are visiting." And to prove he was correct, the angel walked over to one of the boys and called him by name. The boy looked up.

Ellen knew him at once. It was one of Mrs. Brown's children. The boy was entirely unaware of his unseen visitors. The angel began to have an effect on the boy's thoughts, urging him to leave the place at once and to give his life to God. Ellen had been a positive influence for God in his home, and the boy knew full well what the angel was talking about.

With this, the vision vanished, and Ellen was alone again in her room. She sat staring into space, thinking about what she had just seen. Ellen knew what she must do.

With pen and paper in hand, she sat down to write. It was a long, detailed letter to Martha's mother and to her children about the vision. She told what she had seen, offering suggestions to help correct the situation. She also outlined a way these suggestions could be carried out. She was fully aware that the lives of these young people were at stake. Satan was working hard trying to destroy each one of them. Ellen also made a decision to wait and send the letter to them after her return to Wellington, which she did.

Ellen had enjoyed a pleasant time at Long Point with the Brown family. It had been refreshing, for she had seen a delightful, happy family that was more than gracious to her. They also seemed pleased that she led out in morning and evening worship. They listened to what she said and were not turned off.

"I labored with the family," she said, "every morning and night."[3]

Following the vision and writing her letter to the Browns, Ellen felt it was time for her to leave.

But Friday was a very wet day with heavy rain. The worst of the storm had passed, but the road was still muddy. Nevertheless, the trap was made ready for Ellen's and Emily's departure. With a heavy sigh of relief, Ellen felt she was on her way at last. The rain never let up as they reached the station. The little trap was open, so the ladies had to cover themselves with large pieces of burlap to keep dry.

The station had no shelter. So they sat waiting as the rain poured down. Two hours went by, then word came that there would be no train. A landslide had prevented it from coming. So back to the house the two ladies went for the weekend. They would leave on Monday.

What was Ellen's reaction? "We decided," she wrote, "our work was not done and felt reconciled to the delay."[4]

Sabbath, August 5, was a high day in the Brown's home. The little group had its own church service, starting at eleven o'clock and ending about two in the afternoon. The soon-coming Saviour, the shortness of time, and the Sabbath question were the topics. Ellen presented it all, making strong appeals to family members to accept God's way of life.

Ellen went to bed early on Sunday night, August 6. The angel came again. This time at one o'clock in the morning. The angel urged Ellen to make a direct appeal to each of the children. She was to ask them, one by one, to accept God as their guide and Jesus as their personal Saviour.

She did that very thing on Monday morning at worship. Calling each member by name, she pled earnestly with them.

Bell (Isabelle), a beautiful girl of twenty-two, seemed to be the accepted leader for all the other children. It was easy to be around her. She was full of life, fun, and loved parties and dances. The others automatically looked to her with respect.

Ellen asked Bell to make a change from the lifestyle she was living. And when Ellen asked her, "Will you give your heart to Jesus?" Bell answered, "I will!"

Alex was next. He was sixteen and the only boy living at home. He had a keen, quick mind and was a great help to his mother and the family. Ellen turned to him asking, "Will you this very morning choose to be a child of God and engage to serve the Lord Jesus to the best of your ability?"[5]

Without hesitation he answered, "I will."

Victoria was a grown-up lady of fourteen. She had sat quietly listening to everything that was going on. Then looking at her, Ellen asked, "Jesus says to you this morning, 'Victoria, follow Me.' Will you obey His voice?"

Again came the answer, "I will."

Charlotte, the cook for the family, sat listening and watching everything. She was deeply moved. Turning to her, Ellen said, "I am sure you wish to be a child of God." Again, the answer was "Yes."

Prayer followed this moving scene. Emily, Ellen, and others prayed. That very morning the little hilltop house, overlooking the sea, was dedicated to God.

Quietly, and to herself, Ellen gave a great sigh of relief. She was happy and grateful, too, for it was clear now that God had wanted her to be at that house. He not only wanted her to have a vacation, but He wanted to use her to His glory as well.

When she had entered that home a few days earlier, two people were following God. Now, when she was leaving, four more were added to the list. It had taken a vision, a heavy rain, and a windstorm, plus a dedicated little woman to accomplish a great victory for God.

Marriages came to those children as time passed, and more children were added to the Brown family. Among the grandchildren were ministers, editors, and teachers—all belonging to the

Seventh-day Adventist Church. And to think, it all happened because of a much needed minivacation!

Now returning to August 7, we find Ellen, Emily, and Martha Brown ready to leave for the train. They thought that if they watched the weather closely, they could make it to the station and the train between showers.

Did they make it?

"We did," wrote Ellen. Then she added the word, "*almost*."

What was the return trip like?

Ellen White tells us.

"Bedding and trunks got wet, but the train was on time. The second-class car was full, and men were lighting their pipes." (Ellen was allergic to tobacco smoke). The three ladies felt they must find another place to ride. As a result, they were allowed to ride in the freight car. So astride her spring seat, which she always carried with her, and sitting in a freight box with her bedding roll at her feet, Ellen White was quite comfortable. There was a box of dogs nearby, some rather smelly fish, and plenty of boxes of freight. At other stops they were joined by more passengers, until seven women, sitting on boxes of freight and about as many men standing, went rolling through the countryside. "We were thankful to get home anyway," she wrote, "after making this third trial."[6]

Thus ended Ellen White's minivacation on the North Island of New Zealand.

─────────────

1. Arthur L. White, *Ellen G. White: The Australian Years, 1891-1900,* 4:100.
2. Ibid.
3. Ibid., 101.
4. Ibid, 103.
5. Ibid., 101, 102.
6. Ibid., 104.

CHAPTER FIVE

Will 1893 Ever End?

*T*ents were arriving from Australia for Wellington's first-ever camp meeting. The year was still 1893, and the opening date for camp meeting was November 23. Of course, November is summer in New Zealand and a great time for a camp meeting. There was a beehive of activity going on among the church members, with Ellen right there in the middle of it. A camp-meeting site was found outside the city yet close enough for people to walk to it.

The Adventists had to consider two things as they began their evangelistic work. One was prejudice from several groups in the city, including church leaders. They had warned their members against "those Adventists." "Stay away from them," they thundered.

If that wasn't bad enough, the second problem could even be worse. The weather. There was good reason to worry. In Wellington, Ellen warned it was possible that "the wind would strip them [the tents] to ribbons."[1] She wasn't just being pessimistic. A circus had been in town earlier, and high winds had torn the tents to shreds. But this was not a circus; it was an Adventist camp meeting, and the church members felt sure that God would take care of the weather. Many sincere prayers were sent heavenward about wind—and about the prejudice.

Camp meeting was a new thing "down under," and people came from far and near just to watch. Many came with advice and opinions about almost everything. They also asked about a strange ship riding at anchor in the harbor. They knew it belonged to "these people with the tents." Their curiosity reached new heights when they saw officers and crew from the ship working alongside the others getting ready for camp meeting. The Adventists were the talk of the city. The ship's name, it was learned, was *Pitcairn*, and it was a missionary ship. Then the people heard an announcement that the ship's doctor, M. G. Kellogg, would conduct a series of health lectures when the camp meeting began.

And there was something else. Ellen's sixty-sixth birthday took place during camp meeting. And how did she celebrate? She preached. She told her congregation that she and the other speakers were Seventh-day Adventists, and she gave reasons for her faith. She took a direct approach to a sticky subject hoping to break down prejudice, and it seemed to work. There was good attendance every evening, and it grew as the meetings continued. Some came because it was a novelty to hear a woman speak—in fact, something almost unheard of in Ellen White's day. And there she was with that "foreign accent" of hers. But the people came night after night.

Ellen was usually well aware of the makeup of her audiences. She knew who was listening and who was not. She also looked for certain people she or her helpers could work with personally. This is why, from the very first, she noticed that someone she expected to be there was not. None of the Brown family from Long Point came to the camp meeting. This bothered Ellen. It remained so heavy on her mind that she decided to do something about it. Busy as she was, she still took time to write to Mrs. Brown. She urged her to stop whatever she was doing and come to camp meeting. "Be sure and bring the younger members of the family," she wrote. "You will never regret the expense or the trouble."[2]

Did the Brown family show up?

Ellen later wrote her son Edson about what happened. Mrs. Brown not only came to camp meeting, she brought her son Alex and two of her youngest daughters, aged fourteen and nine. All three children were baptized.

Ellen was pleased, but she was surprised with what happened next. Actually, she was confused. All at once, Mrs. Brown and the children left the camp in a hurry. They went home.

The reason for their leaving became clear later when Mrs. Brown showed up again with four of her older girls! She had gone home to get them for the closing days of the camp meeting. In this way, all of the children were able to attend. Was the effort worth it? The four older girls were also baptized!

Ellen was elated, and she reported by letter to Edson. "They [the Browns] have a church now at Long Point . . . numbering nine of their own household."[3]

After the hectic days of camp meeting had ended, an account of the meetings appeared in the *Bible Echo,* January 8, 1894. The *Bible Echo* was a church paper from "down under." The report of this first camp meeting in Wellington rejoiced in "the success of the meetings and its far-reaching influence." Twenty-four people had been baptized and joined the Seventh-day Adventist Church!

Ellen was now ready to return to Australia. She had worked hard in New Zealand, spending all of her time on North Island. Besides her usual aches and pains, she thought back to the ordeal with her teeth and also about her troublesome hip. New Zealand had taken much of her energy, but she was happy in spite of it all. God had been right there with her all the time.

What was waiting for her in Australia? Another camp meeting—this time in Melbourne. It was to start January 5, only a few weeks away. So for Ellen, it was back to packing again, and she knew how to do that.

Before she left, it was decided that two men should remain behind in Wellington to follow up interests created by the camp meeting. One was Dr. Kellogg, from the ship *Pitcairn*. He would join Ellen White later in Australia.

Thus the busy year of 1893 came to a close.

---

1. Ellen G. White, "An Appeal for the Australian Field," *Review and Herald*, no. 48, 70:1.
2. Arthur L. White, *Ellen G. White, The Australian Years: 1891-1900*, 4:110.
3. Ibid., 111.

CHAPTER SIX

When Phineas Came to Town

*P*hineas who? Where did he come from? And how does he fit into the story of Ellen White? Let's keep those questions in mind for the time being, as we jump back to the year 1877. Then we will discuss the fabulous Phineas B.

In 1877, Rutherford B. Hayes was president of the United States. It was Hayes who ordered the last of the federal occupation troops to leave the southern states. Carpetbaggers were fleeing north, and the South was delighted. Carpetbaggers were northern politicians, or adventurers, who had gone south to take advantage of the unsettled conditions following the American Civil War. In Hayes, the southern states now felt they had a real friend in the White House.

The rest of the country found itself plagued with labor troubles. Forty thousand miners went on strike in the nation's coal fields. In Chicago, a violent strike turned into a bloody massacre. Gold and silver workers struck in the far west. And the Baltimore and Ohio Railroad strike exploded into violence.

In 1877 Thomas Edison patented his phonograph, and Brigham Young died on August 29. Also, with the year 1877 came the one-hundredth anniversary of the United States' flag, thus establishing flag day.

This, too, was the year when Chief Joseph led the Nez Perce people on a desperate flight to Canada and lost. The chief surrendered on October 5, only thirty miles from the international border. He gave up to save the lives of women, children, and his warriors. They were in terrible condition and dying of starvation.

"At the time of the surrender," wrote a young lieutenant by the name of Wood, "the able bodied warriors were surprisingly few, in contrast to the number of sick, aged and decrepit men and women: blind people, children, babies and wounded that poured out of their burrows in the earth as soon as it was known that they could do so with safety."[1]

At the surrender the chief uttered these famous words, "Joseph will fight no more forever." Following this he pulled his blanket across his face, "after the fashion of Indians when mourning or humiliated," continued the letter from Wood, "and, instead of walking toward his own camp, walked directly into ours, as a prisoner."[2]

Now, let's talk about Phineas. Who was he? He was Phineas Taylor Barnum, known to millions as P. T. Barnum, the great American showman.

One writer stated that "Barnum was a most typical American without becoming an average American."[3] The elusive world of Barnum was filled with fakes, hoaxes, the sensational, money, and great dreams of illusion. He was master of it all.

When Barnum spoke, people believed him. He actually sold tickets to people to see George Washington's nurse! He said she was one hundred sixty years old. Yet when she died, an autopsy revealed her to be no more than eighty years old. Newspapers had a field day, but Barnum just rode out the storm and then went on to his next sensation. And the public flocked to him again. He imported one of the sacred white elephants of Siam at a cost of $75,000. Siam's king would never allow one of his elephants out of the country. So how did Barnum get one? He used bribery. It took fifteen men, a boat, and gallons of red and blue paint to camouflage and smuggle the beast out of the country.

Not to be outdone, a rival circus owner painted his own elephant with buckets of whitewash. He then declared his elephant one of the sacred white elephants of Siam and branded Barnum's elephant a fraud! Circus-goers knew better, but they didn't care. They loved it—and bought tickets!

Barnum is quoted as saying, "There's a sucker born every minute."[4]

Pestered constantly for free passes to his circus, Barnum had "passes" printed and handed them out to those who asked for them. They read like this:

"Suffer not a man to pass." Judges 3:28.
"The wicked shall no more pass." Nahum 1:15.
"None shall pass." Isaiah 34:10.
"This generation shall not pass." Mark 13:30.
"Beware that thou pass not." 2 Kings 6:9.
"There shall no strangers pass." Joel 3:17.
"No man may pass through because of the beasts." Ezekiel 14:15.
"Though they roar, yet can they not pass." Jeremiah 5:22.
"So he paid the fare thereof and went." Jonah 1:3[5]

But how does P. T. Barnum, showman, figure in the story of Ellen White, God's messenger? Let's watch the day P. T. Barnum rolled into Battle Creek, Michigan. He had his great circus and menagerie with him. But he didn't figure on Ellen White. She was ready for him. So was the Women's Christian Temperance

Union, Doctor John Harvey Kellogg, the Battle Creek Reform Club, church leaders, school officials, and the mayor.

In every issue for almost a month, the *Battle Creek Journal* had a advertisement covering one-third of an entire page announcing the circus. THE GREATEST SHOW ON EARTH was coming to Battle Creek for one day and one day only!

There was to be a great procession with huge elephants and monster lions that obeyed the European Empress of the Dens, M'lle Dumas.

Tickets were fifty cents; children under nine, half-price. For only fifty cents, you could see Captain Costentenus, the tattooed Greek nobleman, a Pigmy named Admiral Dot, the only living hippopotamus in America, and direct from Paris, the lady with the iron jaw, M'lle Millie DeGranville.

But wait! Here come the town fathers and Ellen White.

The Michigan Conference of Seventh-day Adventists gave permission to use its large camp meeting tent. It seated 5,000 people, and the Battle Creek Adventists set it up in plain sight of the Barnum show.

The day the circus came to town, the *Daily Journal* reported, "The crowd at the show this afternoon was immense." Then it went on to add: "The Ladies Temperance dining hall was thronged all day; over 500 took dinner with them. They kept their hall open this evening."[6]

Now, let's look inside the large Michigan Conference tent the day of the circus. Two sources tell us what happened. One is James White's report in the July 5, 1877, issue of the *Adventist Review and Sabbath Herald.* The second is the July 2, 1877, issue of the *Battle Creek Daily Journal.* The *Journal* article reported that inside the Adventist tent "the arrangements for serving refreshments on circus day and meetings on Saturday and Sunday were a remarkable success."[7]

As for the refreshments, you can be sure they weren't serv-

ing 7UP or McDonald hamburgers. Here is what James White had
to say:

Beneath this immense canvas temple were erected
fifteen or twenty tables for the accommodation of guests.
By invitation the Sanitarium of this city erected a large
table in the corner of the great pavilion, which was boun-
tifully supplied with the delicious fruits and vegetables
which constitute the dietary at the institution named. This
table really formed the chief attraction of the entertainment, and was more largely patronized than any other,
notwithstanding the popular prejudice against the hygienic mode of living [what we, today, call "health
food."] Although the table was more than thirty feet in
length, the attraction toward it became so great that it
was necessary to annex another about two-thirds as long,
which was also thronged.

It was really encouraging . . . to see scores of hungry
citizens and country people turning away from the side-
tables [provided by non-Adventists], laden with their fa-
vorite pork and beans, roast beef, salads, tea, coffee, etc.,
and crowding about the Sanitarium table with almost
childlike eagerness to secure a square hygienic meal.
Not a seat was left vacant a moment, and there were
usually a score or two of persons standing behind the
long lines of diners, ready to drop into a seat the instant
it was vacated.

The popular prejudice, usually expressed in such
terms as "bran bread," "starvation diet," and similar epi-
thets, melted away "like mist before the rising sun;" and
words of commendation were on the mouth of everyone. The whole affair was a grand success. More than
one-third of the tickets sold at 25 cents each [just one-

half the admission price to the circus] were taken up at the Sanitarium table. The managers of the table, with their friends, express sincere thanks to the public for the cordial manner in which their effort was received, and the marked attention bestowed upon their table.[8]

According to James White, one of the main reasons behind all this display and effort by the Women's Christian Temperance Union was "to accommodate the crowds of people who gathered in from the country to see the show, and thus prevent them from visiting the saloons and groggeries where they would be exposed to temptation." White added that this "struck a telling blow for temperance and reform."[9]

Handbills were heavily scattered through the crowds going to the great show—and even during the performance itself. The leaflets announced that a temperance mass meeting would be held in the Adventist tent on Sunday, July 1, at 3:00 p.m. and 7:00 p.m.

Saturday night, June 30, found J. H. Kellogg, director of the sanitarium, lecturing in the tent. His talk dealt with the medical and scientific aspects of temperance. He illustrated his remarks with charts and diagrams. He also recounted, by demonstrations, the physical effects of alcohol on the body. The crowd was spellbound as he held them in almost complete silence for well over an hour.

Then on Sunday, July 1, strong winds sprang up in the afternoon, forcing the meeting indoors to the Methodist church. The building was so packed that little or no standing room was left for latecomers. The meeting lasted two hours, with speakers from the Women's Christian Temperance Union and the Battle Creek Reform club. Other speakers included the mayor.

But that was not all. The evening meeting proved to be the climax. A report from the *Battle Creek Daily Journal* of July 2 reported: "In the evening an immense crowd assembled at the tent, more than filling it [the winds had died down by then]; large numbers of persons were obliged to stand on the outside, being unable to gain admittance. It is estimated that 3,000 persons were present."

The paper went on to say that "Elder White [James White] conducted the religious exercises and Mayor Austin presided."

The highlight for the evening was Ellen White herself. "Most of the evening," reported the newspaper, "was occupied by Mrs. White who discussed the question [of temperance] in its relation to the education of children, especially that imparted by mothers."[10]

So far in this chapter, we have briefly touched on a bit of America's past that drew people like a magnet—the great and magical circus world of P. T. Barnum. We have also peeked behind the scenes to view men and women who were clever enough to take advantage of that spectacular event to point people to right living. They did so openly, with refinement and good taste. They hid nothing, even passing out handbills to circus-goers. Plans were well-organized and involved civic leaders, church dignitaries, the mayor, and especially Seventh-day Adventists and sanitarium workers.

Ellen White was recognized as a powerful speaker and a leading force in the cause of temperance. She had an iron will, yet she was a friendly woman with an ancient formula for happiness—the truth of simple living. Ellen White possessed an enormous amount of common sense, which caught people's attention. And when she spoke, people listened.

As that evening of July 1, 1877, arrived and Ellen stepped to the speaker's platform, three thousand listeners fell silent. And when she finished, most of that vast audience were in full agreement with what she said. Her words had taken root in their minds, no matter how pointed she was.

No one recorded her speech stenographically that night. But the temperance message was not new to her, and many of her other talks on that subject have been preserved. Her approach was simple and direct. It focused on home, children, and the duty of parents, mainly mothers.

Here are portions of a temperance message she gave two years later:

> When we take any course which decreases our strength, expends our vitality, beclouds the intellect, and destroys the powers of the mind, we sin against God. In pursuing this course we are not glorifying Him in our bodies and spirits which are His; but we are committing a great wrong in His sight. . . . Those who have preserved their bodies, and their spirits, in holiness, and in sanctification, and honor, will then receive the finishing touches of immortality.
>
> We embrace the truth of God with our different organizations, and as we come under the influence of truth, it will accomplish the work for us which is necessary to be accomplished, and give us a moral fitness for the kingdom of glory, and for the society of heavenly angels. We are now in God's workshop.
>
> When we have tried to present to the people the health reform, and have spoken of the importance of their eating and drinking, and in all that they do, to do it to the glory of God, many, by their actions, have said, "It is nobody's business whether I eat this or that. Whatever we do we are to bear the consequences ourselves."[11]

And from another talk on temperance we have the following:

> God must be made first and last and best in everything. We are to be as teachable as a little child, moving carefully and with entire trust in God. Our eternal interests are involved in the steps we take, whether we move

heavenward toward the city whose maker and builder is God, or earthward toward Sodom's beautiful attractions.[12]

There was great prejudice against Adventism in the early days of the movement. But with the firm, yet gentle touch of Ellen White and others like her, things began to change. Such incidents as that which took place in the Adventist tent during the great circus helped to still the waters of resentment. Adventists were slowly being accepted. An example of this appeared in the *Battle Creek Daily Journal* of July 2, 1877. In the middle of a long, glowing report about the city of Battle Creek itself, mention was made of the church population in the city and this comment was included: "There being some half-dozen or more churches of different denominations, including the church of the Advents [Adventists]. The Advents," continued the article, "have also a college and health institute here, and make this [town] their headquarters."[13] It is of note that no other denomination was mentioned by name in that glowing report on the city of Battle Creek, Michigan.

It seemed that as the Adventists' star of recognition began to rise, others, such as that of Barnum, began to fade. There were others, too; for instance, Buffalo Bill and his wild west show. "Reporters began hailing the Wild West [show] as the 'best open-air show ever seen' and praising Bill as the showman who 'out-Barnumed Barnum.' "[14] Yet in time the wild west show, too, faded out of sight.

It took James White to bring this into a right perspective. He wrote an article in the *Review and Herald* on the temperance meeting of July 1 that seemed to sum it up well: "A deep impression is made upon this community, and Mr. Barnum's big show seems quite forgotten."[15]

And so it went.

---

1. *The American Heritage Book of Indians,* 361.
2. Ibid.

3. M. R. Werner, *P. T. Barnum* (London: Jonathan Cape, 1923), vii.

4. Ibid., viii.

5. Ibid., 320.

6. *Battle Creek Daily Journal*, July 2, 1877.

7. Ibid.

8. James White, *The Review and Herald*, July 5, 1877.

9. Ibid.

10. *Battle Creek Daily Journal*, July 2, 1877.

11. Ellen G. White, "Christian Temperance," *Signs of the Times*, September 18, 1879.

12. Ellen G. White, *Sermons and Talks,* 1:220.

13. *Battle Creek Daily Journal*, July 2, 1877.

14. *This Fabulous Century, 1870-1900,* (New York: Time-Life Books), 266.

15. James White, *The Review and Herald,* July 5, 1877, 12.

CHAPTER SEVEN

Wall
of Fire

S everal times when Ellen White wrote about angels, she used the term "Wall of Fire." For instance, in calling attention to the qualities of the righteous, she wrote, "Angels are attracted to them, and love to linger about their path. . . . Heavenly angels bend lovingly over them and are as a wall of fire round about them."[1] What a great thought! To think that God's angels stand as blazing flames of fire surrounding, guarding, and directing God's followers.

A few years ago I flew to Europe taking my parents with me. I met Mother and Dad in New York City, and from there we flew across the Atlantic. An hour into the flight I smelled kerosene. Flight attendants rushed back and forth along the aisles. Lights blinked off and on several times. Then things seemed to settle down. Earphones were handed out free of charge. This was to calm passengers. Next, a movie flashed on a screen ahead of us. But instead of viewing a movie, all were amazed as we sat watching flames being projected! I turned to look at the projector. It was on fire, amid clouds of smoke! The fire was quickly put out, ear phones collected, and the cabin lights turned off. We were now supposed to go to sleep.

Other than that, the flight went well. I learned later that our plane, which was to continue on to Egypt after landing in Rome, was grounded in Rome. It went no farther.

While on that night flight above the ocean, I had an uneasy feeling. There was nothing below but water, and I thought, "What if . . . ?" Yet, hadn't I prayed before the flight? Yes, I had. I began to relax. I looked out my window into the dark. And as I looked downward, I knew we were not alone. I saw lights. They stretched as far as I could see, one after another. They were ships, lots of ships. I smiled, people were down there, and I felt safe. God had assured me that all was well.

About sunrise, land appeared. As the plane flew over it, I saw the brightest green I had ever seen; it had to be Ireland. There is no other green in the world like it. Next came France, with the great city of Paris spread out below us. We crossed the sparkle of Lake Geneva and the Alps. Then before I knew it, we were landing in Rome. We made it, burned up movie and all!

Riding in a taxi on the streets of that ancient city was unreal to me. Things I had seen in books popped up in front of me. I was spellbound as I looked at the Coliseum.

But it was the day we traveled by train to Florence, Italy, that will always live in my memory.

It was early evening when we arrived in the city. The traveler's aid station was closed, but a listing of hotels was pasted on the window. Glancing down the list, I selected one and hailed a taxi. We were off. I knew I had to get Dad to a bed soon. He was feeling sick from the long train ride. Mother looked and acted exhausted, too. They were not young, but they were brave travelers. And I knew it was up to me to take care of them.

When we arrived at the hotel, I asked Mother and Dad to stay in the lobby. They could relax in the soft, comfortable seats while I went to the second floor and registered. I had noticed while in the taxi that the city was unusually crowded. People were everywhere. Then the woman at the hotel desk told me they had no rooms available—nor did any other hotel in the city. I began to panic. She told me there was a huge convention in the city and every hotel was filled to overflowing. What could I do now? The woman only shook her head.

I went back to the lobby and put on an act for Mother and Dad. They were comfortable for the moment but tired and worn. Dad, I noticed, seemed to be a little more sick than when I had left him.

I smiled, acted happy, and said, "This place is full, but you just sit here while I go down the street to another hotel for rooms." They looked concerned, but I assured them that everything was fine and that I would be back soon.

I went out into the crowded streets of Florence and almost cried. I went a short distance then stopped walking. Where was I going? I didn't know. People were all around me as I said, almost out loud but to myself, "Lord, I need help, and I need it now!"

No sooner were the words out of my mind when I heard a strong, clear voice say, "Go straight ahead!"

I turned instantly to see who was talking to me—especially in English. There was no one there except the passing crowd. Who had spoken to me?

Dazed, I walked straight ahead. Then, just before I reached the next cross street, that same clear voice spoke again. It said, "Turn left." I looked behind me. But just as before, there was nothing to see but the noncaring crowd on the move. None of them were speaking to me.

I turned left.

I had walked about half a block down that street when the same voice spoke to me a third time. It said, "Look up."

This time I didn't turn around. I knew there was no one to

see. So I followed the instructions and looked up. And as I did, I saw a very large hotel. The name on the sign was *Baglioni*. I crossed the street and went into the building.

A pleasant man, who understood and spoke English, was behind the desk. He listened very patiently to the story of my two very tired and sick parents and the need for rooms.

Then came the crisis as I asked. "Do you have any rooms?"

"We have only one room left," was the reply.

"But there are three of us," I answered.

He smiled and to my utter amazement said, "It is a room for three."

Do I believe in angels and a wall of fire? You bet I do. Dad had a good, sound sleep that night, and on the following morning the three of us were rested, refreshed, and ready to continue our journey. I knew we were not alone.

Let's look at that angel wall of fire as it occurred at another time and in another place.

In the mid-1950s a teenage boy walked into the folding department of Pacific Press in Mountain View, California. He was going to work, as he did every day, after school.

"Hi," he called to a man working a large paper-cutting machine. The man smiled but said nothing.

The boy shuddered as he watched the machine's blade slice through a stack of paper. The huge knife was so fast, powerful, and sharp it could cut through anything in its path—even fingers, hands, or arms!

I wouldn't work on that machine for anything, the boy thought.

Time passed quickly as the two went about their work—the boy and the man operating the paper cutter. A space of about five to seven feet separated them.

Suddenly the boy froze in fear at what he saw and heard. His eyes grew big with terror as he watched the man.

Two short clicks was all he heard, but that was enough. They came from the giant cutter. This meant that the blade was coming down. And the man who was working the machine was too horrified to move. His face was as white as snow. He screamed, "Oh, dear God!" Both his arms were beneath the falling blade!

Without warning the boy felt himself being shoved violently aside. And with lightning speed he saw the figure of a man grab the worker at the paper cutter. With powerful arms he yanked the machine operator backward barely ahead of the falling blade. All this happened within the brief fraction of a second.

The man and boy found themselves hurled against a tall stack of printed material. It flew across the room. Both were stunned as they lay on the floor facing each other. Tears rolled down the face of the man as he felt both his arms with trembling fingers. Over and over again, he was repeating, "Thank You, dear Lord. Thank You, dear Lord." There wasn't a scratch on him.

The boy spoke. "Who was that man who saved you?"

Glassy eyed, the man stared back as he stammered, "I don't know."

"Look!" shouted the boy as he pointed at the wall.

Blood drained from both their faces as they stared at the brilliant, glowing shape of a figure passing slowly through the wall. It left a shining hole, and they both could see through it to the room beyond.

"It's an angel," whispered the man. "It's the shape of an angel."

By now, people had heard the commotion and came running. "*Look!*" the two on the floor shouted as they pointed at the wall. But there was nothing there. The hole was gone.

In telling what had happened, the man remembered that once he had been pulled away from the machine, he felt the gentle touch of a hand on his shoulder, followed by a soft pat. "I felt peace," he said, "and a feeling that it was all right now. It was OK."

Now let's talk about fire—not a wall of fire provided by angels but the kind of fire that burns things up.

For the Seventh-day Adventist Church, the years between 1902 and 1906 can be called "the fire years." February 18, 1902, the world-famous Battle Creek Sanitarium burned down. December 30, 1902, saw the Review and Herald Publishing Association destroyed by fire. And then on July 20, 1906, the Pacific Press Publishing Association went up in flames.

"Why?" came the question loud and clear from thousands of church members.

For one answer, let's turn to Isaiah:

> "The Lord said, 'These people claim to worship me, but their words are meaningless, and their hearts are somewhere else. Their religion is nothing but human rules and traditions, which they have simply memorized. So I will startle them with one unexpected blow after another. Those who are wise will turn out to be fools, and all their cleverness will be useless' " (Isaiah 29:13, 14, Good News Bible).

Following the Pacific Press fire, Ellen White thought of a time when the publishing houses pleased God. She said, "I have seen the angels of God passing from room to room, noting the articles that were being published, noting every word and action of the workmen. Their faces were lighted with joy, and their hands were outstretched in blessing."[2]

But all of that changed.

Ellen wrote about the Review and Herald fire on April 14, 1903:

> Pernicious matter has been published right in our office [the same could also be said of the Pacific Press], and if some part of the work had to be delayed, it was

the work on the books containing the light of truth. This was greatly displeasing to the Lord. . . . God desired that every movement should be in accordance with Bible principles. There was to be no sharp dealing. But there has been sharp dealing, and God has been displeased. For the last twenty years God has been sending reproofs and warnings regarding this.[3]

Continuing, she wrote: "Wrongs have been done in the institution [the Review and Herald] but it is not my place to mete out punishment. The Lord has taken this matter in His own hands."[4]

We learned how God felt. But what was her own personal reaction to the destruction of these institutions of the church? These were the very things that she herself worked so hard to help establish. She loved them. They were part of her life. How did these fires affect Ellen White?

Before the fire came which swept away the Review and Herald factory, I was in distress for many days. I was in distress while the council was in session, laboring to get the right matter before the meeting, hoping, if it were a possible thing, to call our brethren to repentance, and avert calamity. It seemed to me that it was almost a life and death question. It was then that I saw the representation of danger—a sword of fire turning this way and that way. I was in an agony of distress. The next news was that the Review and Herald building had been burned by fire, but that not one life had been lost. In this the Lord spoke mercy with judgment.[5]

In an article in the *Review and Herald* George Butler wrote about his conversation with Ellen White following the sanitarium fire. This is some of what he had to say:

We were out looking at the flowers together by ourselves, and I said to her, "Sister White, were you ever
shown anything about the burning of the sanitarium?"
She looked down for a moment, and said, "Brother Butler, I do not wish to talk on this subject." I afterward
learned that she said that she thought the Review and
Herald would go first.[6]

Not long after the great San Francisco earthquake of 1906,
Ellen White was at the Pacific Press in Mountain View, California. The press had damage from the quake and was being repaired
at the time. This is some of what she had to say as she spoke to the
workers:

> While at St. Helena, again and again it has been re-
> vealed to me that there was not a correct state of things
> at Mountain View; that there were present the very con-
> ditions that made it essential for the publishing work to
> be removed from Oakland [Pacific Press had moved from
> Oakland to Mountain View in 1904]. I saw that in the
> working out of human ideas and plans there was a disre-
> garding of the light God had given in the past to correct
> existing evils. There is a danger that the experience of
> the past will be repeated. The men who are serving in
> the management of the work can just as surely swerve
> the work into lines of commercialism as in the past.
> My instructor said, "This in no case must be." There
> have been warnings in the past over and over again, for
> eighteen or twenty years, but we have not fully heeded
> these warnings.

As her talk continued, she spoke directly to many who were
sitting in front of her, not using names but referring to them. She

said, "They are no more with God than those who make no profession of godliness. There are worldlings who scorn to do many things that those who claim to be Christians are doing. The Lord calls for a halt."

In conclusion she stated, "As the light has come to me on many points, I thought perhaps if I could write it out and send it, it would have the same result as for me to stand before you in person. But I am weary of bearing testimonies when I do not see that it brings anything to pass."[7]

The story continues:

In June a letter arrived [at Pacific Press] for the directors, a warning from Ellen White. Commercial work must cease at once or worse calamities would follow.

Alas, dedicated men do not always enjoy the courage of their convictions. The directors agreed not to solicit commercial business; they would accept only work they were asked to do. They did not believe they could limit the Press to God's work alone.

And the Press burned down.

The fire started around midnight on Friday, July 20, 1906. No one ever found out how. No watchman worked that night.[8]

M. C. Wilcox, editor of the *Signs of the Times*®, wrote a letter to the editor of the *Review and Herald*. It was published on August 2, 1906. He begins:

Dear Brother: How can I write the sad news? Yesterday afternoon at the close of a week of hard labor, many of the employees in the Pacific Press left for campmeeting in Oakland, to remain over Sabbath, a few to stay through the meeting. Others went to their homes to rest. A number met together to study the Sabbath-school lesson. All retired to rest with no thought of danger or trouble.

But at twelve o'clock the fire-alarm of our little town

sounded a clamorous appeal. Little did any one think that it was the splendidly equipped Pacific Press plant. . . .

No fire hydrant was nearer the office than two blocks, and with only seven hundred and fifty feet of hose, but one stream could be played on the fire. Our own tanks were useless, as the tank-house was afire. . . . Pine floors and roof and paper fed the voracious element, and soon the whole building was a ruin, roof in, and paper and timbers burning fiercely. . . .

By brave strenuous work seven typewriters were saved and several desks, and some books and files. The mailing lists [stencils] of the *Signs of the Times* and *Our Little Friend* were lost, but we hope that we have a tolerable list in Brother Tait's desk which was saved.[9]

As far as I know, there is no one left today who was there the day the Pacific Press burned. However, a few years ago I was talking to someone who was there. He told me that according to some reports, someone sighted a strange glow above the roof of the building just before the fire broke out. The glow, he said, was not from fire. It was more like a light in the sky. Next came the flames. Some believed that the glow was that of an angel.

There seems to be somewhat of a mystery about these fires that engulfed Adventist institutions. They are difficult to explain or solve. They completely destroyed the buildings until there was nothing left of them, but in all these fires only one person lost his life (when the Battle Creek Sanitarium burned). And it was impossible to put the fires out once they started.

The remarks of Battle Creek's fire chief at the time of the fires are interesting. *The Review and Herald* said of the fire chief: "He had fought every one of the Adventist fires [remember there were two in Battle Creek] and his score was zero. 'There is something strange,' he said, 'about your SDA fires, with the water poured on acting more like gasoline.' "[10]

On May 9, 1903, the church at Battle Creek received a long written statement from Ellen White. It stated plainly that the Review and Herald fire was a judgment from God. This letter, read before the church, did have some effect. Yet not everyone agreed with her. Before printing her words in the *Review and Herald* magazine, the editor of that publication announced before the entire congregation that "at the recent meeting of the stockholders of the Review and Herald the statement was reiterated before a public audience that these fires [that destroyed the Review and the Sanitarium buildings) were not the judgments of God."[11]

Here are parts of her long letter to the Battle Creek church. Keep in mind that it was read in the very church building that also would eventually burn to the ground itself and that not all who heard it accepted what she had to say.

I am bowed down and greatly troubled. I am in sore distress. My whole being is full of pain. At times it seems to me that I can not live. The thought of the terrible spiritual destitution among our people presses heavily upon me. God's judgments have fallen upon our institutions in Battle Creek; but how little has this done to move hearts to repentance! Must the rebuke of God still continue to be felt? And will it still continue to be without effect? I am amazed at the apparent indifference of many who should see and understand. I know not what to say or do. Seeing that the judgments of God have made so light an impression on the minds of those occupying important positions, fear and trembling take hold of me as to what will be the next revelation of God's displeasure.

Men have dishonored God by choosing their own way. . . .

Strong, hard words flowed from her pen. She was not only

speaking from her heart but for God Himself. She continued:

> Those who have disregarded the messages of warn-
> ing have lost their bearings. Some, in their self-confidence,
> have dared to turn from that which they knew to be truth,
> with the words, "Who has told Sister White?" These
> words show the measure of their faith and confidence in
> the work that the Lord has given me to do. They have
> before them the result of the work that the Lord has laid
> upon me, and if this does not convince them, no argu-
> ments, no future revelations, would affect them.

This was followed by a warning. "The result," she said, "will
be that God will speak again in judgment."

But even after these powerful words she offered a message
of hope: "Yet His hand is stretched out to save, if thorough repentance is shown."[12]

W. W. Prescott, a member of the Review board, read Ellen
White's letter to the congregation. When he finished he stated, "I
do before God accept this as a rebuke to me in my connection
with it. I have asked for God's forgiveness in this matter."[13]

Prescott maintained that the calamities were God's judgments
regardless of what others might think. He called for a general show
of agreement from the audience, asking those to stand with him
who acknowledged these things. Most stood, but not all.

It took two more fires before the people began to listen to
God's voice through Ellen White.

M. C. Wilcox summed up the situation pretty well: "He [God]
would have us learn that institutions are secondary, and principles
personified in men are primary; that the thing He wants spread
abroad is His mighty gospel message of living principles, not the
fame of institutions; that institutions are of worth, and only of
worth, as they are used to His glory."[14]

Wilcox's closing remark is well worth repeating. "This report," he wrote, "is written on paper fished from the fire. We plead for the prayers of our brethren and sisters in this great and awful calamity. We are of good courage, but we long for the clear leading of God."[15]

Thus, another battle for God was won, but at what a cost!

---

1. Ellen G. White, *The Sanctified Life,* 13.

2. Ellen G. White, Manuscript Release 276 (Silver Spring, Md.: Ellen G. White Estate), 74.

3. Ellen G. White, *Review and Herald,* April 14, 1903.

4. Ibid., August 4, 1903.

5. Ibid., April 14, 1903.

6. Ibid., April 28, 1903.

7. Ellen G. White, Unpublished talk presented in Mountain View, California, May 3, 1906. Pacific Press Board Minutes.

8. Lawrence Maxwell, *Watching for the Dawn,* 6.

9. *Review and Herald,* August 2, 1906.

10. *Review and Herald,* December 8, 1977, 8.

11. *Review and Herald,* May 19, 1903.

12. Ibid.

13. Ibid.

14. Ibid.

15. Ibid.

CHAPTER EIGHT

The Gold Card

*P*owerful beings live, move, and sweep their thundering voices across endless space to praise God. They interact with human beings—protecting, guiding, and influencing. Who are these beings?

Angels.

These beacons of light are filled with deep and devoted love as they bow low to worship the Creator who made them. With every breath they show a burning desire and a keen eagerness to do His will, and His will only. They are swift to carry out His every wish, for their greatest happiness is to please Him. Their aim is to do anything they can to help bring the human race and God back together again.

Yet they never overstep their bounds. They are obedient, loyal, faithful, and well able to carry out their orders from heaven— even, as we have seen, if it means starting a fire!

Some of Ellen White's friends were angels. She knew a few on a personal basis, even recognizing their individual voices. But the angel she knew best was the one who led her through the many visions she had.

I once asked Arthur White, Ellen's grandson, "What did the angel look like who came to see Ellen White in her visions?"

He looked straight at me with a twinkle in his eyes. Then, without hesitation, he told me exactly what the heavenly visitor looked like. I didn't believe him.

A few years passed, however, and I had an opportunity to ask him the same question a second time. He was in my office at Pacific Press. As before, without hesitation, he gave me the same answer he gave the first time. This time I believed what he said— because he had twice told me exactly the same thing. Yet I was so overwhelmed by what he said that I failed to ask him *how* he knew what Ellen's "vision angel" looked like. Later, after Arthur's death, I asked the White Estate in a letter where he had gotten his knowledge on this. The White Estate felt it had been handed down by word of mouth from Ellen to her son Willie to his son Arthur.

Here is what Arthur White told me about the actions and appearance of the angel who came to Ellen White in her visions. He said that many times the angel would wake her up by standing at the foot of her bed. He had entered the room by the door, just like anyone else. He appeared as a young man, tall, well-built, with a nice face, and (this is the part I hesitated to accept the first time Arthur told it to me) *he was dressed like any other well-dressed man that one would see in public.* There were no bright lights around him, no glow, no wings—none of that. He appeared as just a young man on a visit.

I wanted to know more about this angel who appeared to Ellen White in her visions. I felt there had to be more than what Arthur and the White Estate had told me—some additional evidence somewhere. So I began to search through Ellen White's writings themselves. And as a result, I located two references to that angel.

The first one reads:

> While in California, in the year 1874, I was given an
> impressive dream. . . . I dreamed that several of the breth-
> ren in California were in council. . . . Then a young man
> whom I had frequently seen in my dreams came into the
> council. He listened with deep interest to the words that
> were spoken, and then, speaking with deliberation and
> authoritative confidence, said . . .[1]

Let's stop there. What the angel said at this point is not our
focus. But notice several things from this passage about this angel.

First, Ellen White was in a dream. She refers to this angel as
"a young man whom I had frequently seen in my dreams." In the
latter part of her life Ellen mostly had dreams, rather than visions. In her earlier years, by contrast, she had visions while wide
awake, in addition to dreams.

The second thing to notice is that the information the angel
gave was a message of instruction for church leaders. Messages
from heaven came to Ellen White through both means—dreams
and visions. Both were of equal importance (see Acts 2: 17, 18).

The next thing to notice is that she referred to the angel as "a
young man." She also said that she had seen him "frequently." In
her dream, that young man joined the men in their meeting as one
of their members. In other words, the angel looked no different
than they did. He was dressed as they were dressed. He also discussed their subject with knowledge, good sense, and with authority. He held their attention, and they accepted what he had to
say.

Now let's look at the second reference I found regarding this
angel who appeared to Ellen White in her dreams and visions.
This experience took place a year later, in 1875:

Several speakers had addressed large and attentive congregations at the camp meeting in Rome, New York, on first day, September 12, 1875 [in the early days of the church the days of the week were often referred to as first day, second day, third day, and so on, instead of Sunday, Monday, Tuesday]. The following night I dreamed that a young man of noble appearance came into the room where I was, immediately after I had been speaking. This same person has appeared before me in important dreams to instruct me from time to time during the past twenty-six years.[2]

In this passage, we learn that it was the same "young man" who came to see her each time in her dreams and that he had done so with some frequency. Also, during the twenty-six-year period Ellen White mentions, this individual didn't age; he was still a "young man."

And something else. New York is thousands of miles in distance from California, the location of the first reference we looked at. In other words, this "young man" could travel anywhere he pleased at any time. It didn't matter how far the distance was, he could go there. He also knew where Ellen White was at all times.

This brings up the fascinating subject of angel travel. How fast can angels travel? Some people believe angels can travel at the speed of thought. Personally, I believe they can travel even faster than that. Daniel has given us some evidence of how quickly angels can travel. "While I was speaking in prayer, the man Gabriel, whom I had seen in the vision at the first, came to me in swift flight" (Daniel 9:21, RSV). (Notice that Daniel, too, refers to the angel Gabriel as a "man.") Apparently, Gabriel left heaven in answer to Daniel's prayer for further understanding and appeared by his side before Daniel had finished praying! That is traveling quickly indeed.

In studying the subject of atoms, I discovered a startling feature about the movement of these tiny things. I learned that an atom can vanish instantly from one location, only to reappear immediately in another spot *without traveling the distance in between!*[3] What does this tell us? Is this possibly the way angels travel? You be the judge on that one.

But returning to what angels look like—how does Ellen White describe them? Let's find out.

In one of her early visions Ellen had a view of other planets. Her angel friend was with her. In that vision she spoke to those who lived, as she put it, on "other worlds." She wrote:

> The Lord has given me a view of other worlds. The inhabitants of the place were of all sizes; they were noble, majestic, and lovely. They bore the express image of Jesus, and their countenances beamed with holy joy. . . . I asked one of them why they were so much more lovely than those on the earth. The reply was, "We have lived in strict obedience to the commandments of God, and have not fallen by disobedience, like those on earth."[4]

The following headline appeared in the January 9, 1992, *Idaho Press-Tribune*: "New Planets Found in Milky Way."[5] A few days later, the same publication carried this headline: "Scientists: Sorry, no Planet."[6] However, at the end of that second article I found this footnote:

> The Daily Telegraph quoted him [Dr. Matthew Bailes] as saying the error does not invalidate subsequent reports by other astronomers of planets around other stars.
>
> These astronomers did not make the error the Britons made, and it is possible the Milky Way teems with such planets.[7]

From the science magazine *Discover* comes this startling news. The cover story for the September 1997 issue is titled: "Impossible Planets." Four lines of copy on the cover say: "Finally we've found other planets, orbiting other suns. And they're far stranger than anything we ever imagined."

These newly-discovered planets apparently do not act like the planets in our own solar system. They are out there, lots of them, but who in the scientific world can tell us how they work? A subhead in the *Discover* magazine article sums it up by saying, "After decades of searching, we've finally found other planets orbiting other stars, and found them in abundance. Now the only problem is figuring out how on earth to explain them."[8]

Other worlds? Beings from outer space? The Bible says they are out there. So does Ellen White. And as new information continues to come in from powerful telescopes, scientists keep scratching their heads trying to figure it all out.

I found this statement about Ellen White and her relationship with angels in materials put out by the Ellen G. White Estate for Spirit of Prophecy Emphasis Week (1974):

> Angels come to us from an outer-space place called heaven, and the distance from their home to ours is as nothing to them. One second they are there; the next, one of them can be standing right next to us. . . . They can look like ordinary people, or they can appear like sudden flashes of flame, or they can be invisible. They can speak, using our language. Ellen Harmon (White) was a teenager when she saw her first angel in a dream. She described him as "a person of beautiful form and countenance."
>
> Angels often spoke to Ellen White while she was having visions. Sometimes, in vision, they carried her in their arms (*Early Writings*, pp. 20, 32). Often they pro-

tected her from danger. She called her own special guardian angel, "My attending angel" (*Early Writings*, p. 37); "My accompanying angel" (*Story of Redemption*, p. 42); "My guide" and sometimes "the young man."[9]

Now let's turn to Ellen's own words as she describes what the angels she saw really looked like. Angels' faces, she wrote, are "mild and expressive of happiness." Their foreheads are "high and broad, showing a powerful intellect." Their forms are "perfect," and their "bearing noble and majestic."[10]

They wear garments of light, which, at times, can look like heavenly armor. They are taller than Adam and Eve but shorter than Jesus was before He came to this earth. They are real beings, as well organized as any army. Each angel has his assigned place, for there is perfect order in heaven.[11]

> These heavenly beings . . . frequently disguise themselves in the form of human beings, and as strangers converse with those who are engaged in the work of God. In lonely places they have been the companions of the traveler in peril. In tempest-tossed ships they have spoken words to allay fear and inspire hope in the hour of danger. Many [human beings], under different circumstances, have listened to the voices of the inhabitants of other worlds. Time and again have they [angels] been the leaders of armies. They have been sent forth to cleanse away pestilence. They have eaten at the humble board of families, and often have they appeared as weary travelers in need of shelter for the night.[12]

But what about "gold cards," the cards referred to in the title to this chapter?

Who of us is not acquainted with a wallet full of plastic cards?

We have all kinds of them, and they come in different colors. Some even have pictures. We have security cards, I.D. cards, medical cards, and, of course, credit cards. The list is endless. Some credit cards are called "gold cards," but that is not the kind of gold card we are talking about here.

One day while I was reading through some of Ellen's writings, I came across a bit of information that puzzled me. And I found no answer until I began to search for an explanation in other writings by her.

Here is the statement that puzzled me:

> My attending angel directed me to the city again [the Holy City in heaven] where I saw four angels winging their way to the gate of the city. They were just presenting the golden card to the angel at the gate when I saw another angel flying swiftly from the direction of the most excellent glory, and crying with a loud voice to the other angels, and waving something up and down in his hand.[13]

What was happening here? Ellen herself didn't know. Later, she learned that the flying angel had a message to delay the four angels from letting loose the winds of strife on the earth (see Revelation 7:1) until God's people were safely sealed as His own.

So, that explains the swiftly flying angel, but what about those golden cards? What are they all about? That bothered me. "Why," I asked myself, "should there be a need for an I.D. card, or any card, in heaven—especially for entering or leaving the city"?

I kept searching for an answer. And my efforts eventually paid off, because I found this statement: "There is perfect order and harmony in the Holy City. All the angels that are commissioned to visit the earth hold a golden card, which they present to the angels at the gates of the city as they pass in and out."[14]

Here was an answer, and I raised my eyebrows in surprise at

what I read. I must admit, however, that it took a little time for me to accept the fact that angels use identification cards as they leave and reenter the heavenly city. I had never thought of that before. But it did make sense.

Why, I wondered at first, *is there need for security at the gates of the heavenly city? Aren't God's angels perfect, loyal, and above all, powerful and trustworthy? Of course they are. Then what is the need for a card?*

But think about that for a moment. Not all angels are good. There are angels who hate God and who are filled with evil and bitterness toward Him. These are the ones who fell from power as they followed Lucifer and believed his lies. They were tossed out of heaven bodily, never to return. Have any of them ever tried to go back? We know that Satan did—at least once. Were there other times we don't know about? Do these fallen angels still have the ability to approach the city? These are hard questions.

Then another thought came to me. If it were possible, would not those fallen angels try imitating God's loyal angels in order to get back inside the city to cause trouble at the very center of God's headquarters?

Then I noticed something else in that quotation. Apparently, it is only the angels who have business on earth who are required to carry the gold card. Fallen angels, it seems, may yet have the power to approach heaven but are unable to get inside. The golden card evidently can't be counterfeited—if evil forces were to try duplicating one.

Clearly, there must be a definite reason for the card and its use. But what is it? One can only speculate. One reason God's loyal angels, who have business on earth, are required to carry that special identification may be because the earth is Satan's headquarters. Yet even though Satan and his followers have lost much of their strength, they still possess great knowledge and power. They are masters of deception. Angels who go to other places in

God's universe apparently do not need the safety measure of a card. Satan has no access to them, only to angels who come to earth.

Satan is an impostor, and if possible, he could appear as one of God's loyal angels from earth, standing at the gates of heaven holding a card in his hand. But without the right card, his cunning and deception wouldn't work. He cannot get back into heaven. Job 2:1 tells about a time Satan tried to penetrate heaven officially—and failed. It's sad to think that heaven itself must be on constant alert against the powerful forces of evil.

For whatever reason, the golden card exists. It's there, and in vision Ellen White saw the angels use it.

So deadly is the rebellion against God that even heaven must sometimes take measures to guard itself against the forces of evil and the touch of sin. Never forget, even for one second, that the horrible war of destruction that began in heaven is still not finished. It is still being fought and will be with us until the Lord returns.

It is very real. But so are the angels who are ever prepared to help us.

1. *Life Sketches of Ellen G. White,* 208.

2. *Counsels on Health,* 465.

3. Timothy Ferris, ed., *The World Treasury of Physics, Astronomy, and Mathematics* (City, Publisher, and date), Introduction.

4. Ellen G. White Estate, "Spirit of Prophecy Emphasis Week for Seventh-day Adventist Schools, 1974, 10.

5. *Idaho Press-Tribune,* January 9, 1992, 7A.

6. Ibid., January 16, 1992, 5A.

7. Ibid.

8. *Discover,* September 1997, 78.

9. Ellen G. White Estate, "Spirit of Prophecy Emphasis Week for Seventh-day Adventist Schools, 1974, 14-16.

10. *Story of Redemption,* 13.

11. See *Seventh-day Adventist Bible Commentary,* 901.

12. *Story of Redemption,* 37.

13. *Life Sketches of Ellen G. White,* 118.
14. *Early Writings,* 39.

CHAPTER NINE

When Ellen White Laughed

A re God's prophets real people? Do they laugh? Do they cry or get sick? Does it hurt when they fall down? And what about their fingers? When one gets cut or scratched, does it bleed? In short, do God's prophets experience life just like you and I have to do? Let's find out.

One warm, summer day, a happy little lady told me a story about Ellen White. We were at a place called Elmshaven. It is in California, and it was Mrs. White's last home. You should go there if you ever have the opportunity.

The happy little lady who told me the story was Mrs. White's granddaughter. Her name was Grace Jacques.

And this is what she told me.

Way back in the year 1900, Ellen White sailed on a large ship across the Pacific Ocean. Some of her family and friends sailed with her. They got on the ship in Australia and were going all the way to the United States. The children in the group were excited to see how big the ocean was. And they laughed and clapped their hands when they saw fish leaping right out of the water. The fish went high into the air and then back into the water. They saw birds, too, and bright-colored clouds.

Porpoises followed their ship almost like pets on a leash. They swam close to the ship and then veered away only to return, leaping and swerving as they came. They played with the ship as if it were a toy—sometimes in front of the ship, sometimes next to it, and some-times following behind. These beautiful porpoises were having as much fun in the water as were the people watching them from the decks.

At one of the south sea islands, the ship made a stop, and, of course, the passengers wanted to go ashore. But the water was too shallow for the ship to get very close to the land. Yet there was a way for them to get to shore.

And this is how they did it.

As the large ship stayed in deep water, smaller boats took pas-sengers toward the island. But then, even the little boats had trouble. The water was too shallow for them as well.

Now what were they going to do? The people from the ship didn't want to go back. They wanted to see the island.

And so they did.

Natives, big, strong men living on the island, waded out into the water to the little boats. And, one by one, they picked up the passen-gers and carried them to shore.

Mrs. White was lifted from a boat by two of the men with big muscles. They joined their hands together to make a seat for her to sit on, and away they went sloshing through the water. She enjoyed this as she put her arms around those men and hung on tight. She even laughed a little.

Once they had her safely on shore, the men led her to a large rock and sat her on top of it. It was a great place to sit. From her perch on the rock she could watch other passengers being carried to shore.

Suddenly, as she sat watching, she saw Ethel May White, her

son Willie's wife, being carried to shore. A very large, strong native man had picked her up from one of the small boats. All the man wore was a piece of cloth wrapped around his middle. So, you see, he didn't care if he got wet. And after carrying several passengers through the water, he *was* wet, of course, which made his skin slippery. Ethel May was wearing a long dress as ladies did at that time. If she were standing, it would almost touch the floor. Well, she pulled the dress up so it wouldn't get wet and climbed on the back of the native. She wrapped her legs around his slippery middle. One arm went around his neck, and with her other arm she held an open umbrella high above her head.

It was funny to watch. But that was not all.

The man had a hard time going through the water; he almost fell! Ethel May was hanging on so tight she almost choked him. And her legs dug into his middle. He wasn't doing so well. Besides having a woman on his back who was choking him, he had something under his arm. It was a baby, and it was screaming. It was Ellen White's granddaughter (but not Grace Jacques, who was telling me this story).

What a sight to see!

Ellen White, sitting on her rock on the shore, was watching it all. She started to smile. Then she began to laugh softly. Next she laughed out loud. The more she laughed and the more she watched, the noisier her laughter became. She started to laugh so hard that she began to rock back and forth on her rock. Her sides began to hurt from all that laughing. Then she felt herself sliding. Her arms went up in the air. And all of a sudden there was no Ellen White anywhere. She had disappeared!

It was a good thing someone saw her feet sticking up in the air. Because she had fallen off the rock! It was good, too, that she fell on sand, or she might have hurt herself.

People ran to help her. And would you believe it, when they finally got her to stand on her feet again, she was still laughing! But not as hard as before.

Are prophets real people? Sure they are. They are just as real as you and me. They know how to have fun. They laugh when they see something funny. They even cry, get hurt, and do all the other things anyone else does. Yet there is one big difference between God's prophets and us. And we should never forget it, even for one second. The difference is that God gives them messages directly from Himself. He gives us messages *through* His prophets. And the messages God gives us through His prophets, like Ellen White, come right from Him.

They are messages of love, just for us.

---

* This chapter is based on a personal interview with Grace Jacques at Elmshaven, California.

Afterthoughts

N ow that you have read this far in this book, you know that Ellen White was a real human being. Let's take a few more minutes to look at this genuine human side of her life. Of course, she had a special, close connection with God that affected her. Still, she was a real woman, a person who lived in the world of her day just as did anyone else.

Picture this scene if you will. I can imagine it clearly in my mind.

The weather is warm. On the second floor of an old house a breeze causes the curtains to flutter. It is early, so early, in fact, that the sun has not yet reached this part of the world. The big house stands dark and quiet, seemingly empty and alone. There are a few sounds to be heard, but they are not coming from the house—the soft rustle of feathers from a sleepy bird, the far off bark of a dog, and once in awhile the slow flap of wings from a nighthawk or an owl on the move. Other than these, there is nothing more to be heard.

But the curtains in the old house continue to move in an upstairs window. There is no screen, and soft breezes are pushing the curtains soundlessly back and forth, in and out of the window. There had been a light in the room, but it had gone out long before, leaving only darkness. Yet there comes the strong feeling of a presence, of a person watching from behind those curtains. There is no face to be seen, but someone is there.

It seems as if time is standing still. Then, and very slowly, a hand reaches forward to touch the curtains, pulling them aside. A face appears and turns to the east to watch the slow rising of the sun as day, with all its color, begins to spill light across a waking world.

The face is that of Ellen White. It is a gentle, kind face, that has been softened by years of time and hard work. It speaks of battles long since settled. And of others yet to come. Her face, now touched by the morning light, is relaxed, quiet, and content. Her eyes are enjoying something God has made.

As the sun reaches higher and higher, lighting all it touches, Ellen starts to smile. A flood of memories is crossing her mind. She thinks backward to another day and time. "Last night!" she whispers to herself, remembering the Salamanca vision. "Last night," she repeats again. With closed eyes she recalls the day when a room in Battle Creek was filled with people and the strange events that followed.

Next comes the sound of a low laugh. Ellen is picturing Barnum's great white elephant.

She reaches up to feel her mouth, and touching her teeth, she thinks of the New Zealand she loves, and Dr. Karo.

The sun is well up now as she stretches and yawns. She likes doing her work when everyone else is in bed. But this time she has stayed up later than usual and feels extra tired. She also knows that in a few minutes her friend Sara McEnterfer will be in to check on her. She always does. But just for now, things are quiet, and she remembers.

The soft glow of gold from the sun falls across a thousand leaves as they twist and turn in the breeze. The sight brings to her mind the gold cards of heaven—the ones angels carry to and from earth.

Pictures come to her mind faster now. Baby Herbert is once more in her arms. Then there is Henry, her first child, gone at sixteen. Both wait for Jesus to wake them. But for now they must sleep in that small cemetery at Battle Creek. Her eyes fill with tears that run down her face. She thinks of her husband, James, who stood beside her through so many years—resting now and waiting for Jesus' return. And she whispers, half to herself and half aloud, "Please, Jesus, come soon!" She pauses and then adds once more, "Please."

Ellen White lived a long, full, and rich life. At times it was filled with deep sorrow. There was the loss of two sons and a husband. At other times there was joy. And much of that joy came through time spent with her grandchildren. She loved them as they laughed and played with her.

During her long years of service, many of her writings were misunderstood or rejected. She was loved and hated at the same time. She was accused of many things. Her life was even threatened. But through it all Ellen White had a hope. It was a hope founded on her knowledge of a new and better world. Oh, how she longed to go there! Her greatest desire was for Jesus to come back to earth again in His great and glorious second coming. Then and only then would all of God's people be able to go home with Him. Heaven would be their real home, and they would never, ever, have to leave it.

Pain, sorrow, threats on her life, disappointment, hardship, inconvenience, and even sickness never stopped her from doing what God asked her to do. Her work for Him always came first.

While doing research on Ellen's life, I was able to read through most of her diaries and personal papers. They show a human side of Ellen White, that we sometimes fail to realize. Would you like to have a look at a few of the things I found? As we do so, think back to the times in which Ellen lived. It was much different from our day. Ready? Let's go.

Ellen was a social person. People were important to her. Here are three references (among many) from her diaries that tell of contacts she made with people while she traveled—and of her reaction and comments to these encounters.

The first is dated March 8, 1893. The setting is New Zealand. There had been a public meeting in the town of Kaeo. She wrote:

> At the close of the meeting, I was introduced to sev-
> eral [of those attending]. One woman with two little chil-
> dren grasped my hand. She was the sister of Wesley
> Hare's wife. She said, "I was impressed this morning
> that I must take the boat and come down the river to this
> meeting." Her husband was ill, but she left him in the
> care of the children. She brought the baby and the older
> little boy to take care of the baby while she rowed the
> boat six miles. She said, "I was very tired, but oh, how
> glad I am that I came! Oh what a meeting this has been!
> I was never in such a meeting before." She came for-
> ward [when a call was made to accept Jesus], and I know
> that the Lord blessed her. Her husband had expressed
> fears that a storm might come up, and there might be
> another flood. She assured him that she would watch
> every indication of the weather and turn homeward at
> the first sign of a storm.[1]

The second reference happened on board the *Wairarapa*, a ship in the waters off New Zealand. The date was December 19, 1893. A woman stewardess serviced the area of the steamer where Ellen White was sitting. Her diary tells what happened.

The lady in waiting is very kind to me. I gave her *Steps to Christ* and some papers and pamphlets. I talked with her in regard to her soul's salvation. I pointed out the perils of any one whose life was on the sea. She said she had thought of this ofttimes, but she said, "If I could, I would be a Christian, but I cannot. It would be an impossibility to serve God on such a vessel as this. You do not know, you cannot have any idea of the wickedness of these sailors. . . . The captain and mates are so closely of the same character with the crew of sailors that they have no influence to introduce reform if they desired such a thing." I asked why she did not seek some other employment. She said, "It would be no use. I have four children to support and I have not the strength to do hard work." She was a small, delicate, fine-featured woman. "I earn more here on this ship than I could obtain in any other employment."

I tried to open before her the danger of living a prayerless life. She said, "It is no use to pray here, or try to be religious." I told her if the Lord had appointed her that place she would, if she would accept Christ as her Saviour, realize Christ as her refuge. She said, with tears in her eyes, "It is impossible. I know the company on this ship. I could not live religion here. I hope some time to have some place opened for me where I can support my family, and then I shall give my attention to serious things. If I could only be with my children and support them in a humble way I would only too gladly choose to do so."

Later that same day the ship anchored near Auckland. Some of Ellen White's party went ashore in a small boat. In doing so, Emily Campbell was left behind. She became very upset about this and greatly disappointed. The mate of the ship came to her and quieted her down by saying that the boat would return and go back to shore again for another trip. This soothed Emily, and she was happy again.

Now let's continue with Ellen's diary.

> The mate entered into conversation with her [Emily] and told her . . . much the same as the stewardess had said in regard to the wickedness of the sailors and the crew. He said, "I have been much impressed that this boat will go down with all hands on board ere long. I have felt so strongly exercised that I shall not, if I can possibly disconnect from it, continue to remain on the boat."

Ellen wrote more about this later. She added, "This nice boat went down, sank with all on board with the exception of two, in a few weeks after this. The mate was one that was saved. The stewardess nurse was advertised as among the list of the lost. . . . What is to be hoped," she added, "for this class? My heart aches."[2]

And now for the third incident. It took place at Ellen White's home in Australia. The date was Tuesday, June 14, 1898. This is what she wrote in her diary:

> Two tramps, as they are called, came to our house. They were from Sydney. They wanted something to eat. We gave them a breakfast, and they chopped some wood. They afterward had dinner, and in the noon meal we gave them a dish of good hot vegetable soup. They seemed to enjoy it very much. They ate like men who were hungry. We then put them up a loaf of bread and a quart of jam to take with them. They did not look at all like tramps. They were very respectable-looking men. We gave them a roll of reading matter. We thought it might be seed

sown beside "all waters."[3]

Not much escaped Ellen's eyes as she traveled. Her diaries are filled with firsthand observations. While in Basel, Switzerland, for instance, she noticed the role that women played in that place. The date was October 1, 1885.

> We saw two girls about seventeen years old, one on either side of the tongue of a heavy cart like two horses. A large, broad belt was upon the shoulders of one; the other had a strap about her waist. The cart was loaded, and they were dragging it up hill. A stout man and a boy about ten years old were behind pushing. This would be a singular sight in America, but nothing unusual here. Women draw hand-wagons loaded with fruit or vegetables. We purchased a chair in the city. A woman delivered it, carrying it on her head. Women of the medium class go bareheaded in cold weather as well as in warm.[4]

She made a similar observation in Cologne as she observed people on the streets, especially the women. Here again, we read from her diary:

> Now come the market women. There are hundreds of them. They come, young women, middle-aged women, young girls, old women of gray hairs with heavy, loaded baskets upon their heads, full of fruit and vegetables. They bring all kinds of products to market. It is raining and the dresses are tucked up under the waist. One girl of eighteen has loaded herself down completely—a very large basket upon her head, two baskets on one arm, and another with bouquets.[5]

Ellen White was one hundred percent a woman through and through—as the following two references from her diaries will show. Read what she wrote in her diary when she saw a good-looking man. On November 27, 1891, she was on a ship sailing from the United States, bound for Australia. The ship made a stop at the Samoan Islands, as Ellen called them. Natives had come from the islands to the ship in small boats selling fruit, pictures, shells, and souvenirs. These natives would also take passengers in their boats to the islands and back for fifty cents apiece. Ellen did not go ashore. But she recorded in her diary what she observed:

> Here comes stalking by me, as I sit writing on the boat, a large athletic native with a blue jacket and a blue calico cloth about his loins. The natives are, some of them, quite good looking.[6]

Another similar reference appears from a time when she was aboard her son Edson's boat, the *Morning Star,* on the Mississippi River. The date was June 8, 1904.

> A little machine boat was taken along to be used in an emergency and by some accident she filled with water and overturned. Professor Sutherland, Willie White, and my stenographer Clarence soon were in readiness to exchange pants and coat for their very becoming bathing suits. . . ."[7]

Needless to say, the small boat was rescued and uprighted.

Now we come to one of Ellen's pet peeves—noise pollution. She makes numerous references to this problem; I've selected only two. The first is from July 31, 1885. She was staying overnight in the town of Worcester, Massachusetts. "This is a very noisy place, with carriages passing continually. The heavy wagons over the stone pavements make my head ache."[8]

That entry was rather mild compared to this comment from her stay in Europe at Torre Pellice, Switzerland, on April 18, 1886. She wrote: "All is astir in Torre Pellice as early as five a.m., and there is a constant clatter, clatter of big wooden shoes on stone pavements."

Four days later, on the twenty-second, she mentioned the noise again:

> Early in the morning the clatter, clatter, clatter of the wooden shoes forbids sleeping. It is market day. Men, women, and children are rushing over the stone pavements, dragging hand wagons or carrying baskets and bundles on their heads. There is a bright sunshine today, and all are preparing to exhibit their wares in the market place. Here comes a woman with a long stick on her back from which is dangling a dead kid [a young goat]. Two more peasant women with dead kids hanging from a pole on their backs; a woman has a live kid in her arms; a man passes with three dead kids, and now there is a cart full of the same article—kids for market. In the market everything is displayed—dry goods of a very nice quality, socks, yarn, silk handkerchiefs, all kinds of vegetables, and an array of shoes from the finest grade to the most clumsy wooden shoes which go clatter, clatter, clatter, making a deafening sound.[9]

But Ellen was even more agitated at another incident she experienced while in Switzerland—and said so plainly. On July 11, 1886, she was invited to address the workers at the Seventh-day Adventist headquarters in Switzerland, along with others who wished to hear her. Here, in her own words, is what took place.

Within the enclosed yard, within a few feet of the

office and meetinghouse and directly beneath us in the
basement of the building composing the old office, are
premises rented out to a blacksmith, and while services
are being held, there is the ringing of the hammer, the
pounding, and all the noise which can be made in a
blacksmith's shop. So the prayers and preaching and
exhortations on the Sabbath are mingled with the sound
of the hammer and anvil, while in the next apartment is
a marble shop where tombstones and monuments are
manufactured, and there is the sound of the chisel and
hammer upon the granite and marble.

She followed this description with a personal and very pointed
comment, choosing words that reveal an irritation that was meant
to be heard. She wrote, "This has been going on for six years, and
how God can look with any favor upon a people claiming to believe the truth and yet so blinded to the fitness of things seems
incomprehensible to me."[10]

A final reference to noise. This comment was recorded in
two different places and will tell about her frame of mind. The
first is dated February 8, 1893, aboard a ship near Auckland, New
Zealand.

All went off well, but after the supper and the wine
and liquor were indulged in, then we were treated to a
carousal by the rougher class—dancing around the deck,
hallooing, laughing, and singing songs all out of tune
and season. I asked the stewardess if it could not be
stopped. She said it was no use to try. Should the captain make an attempt, they would turn and say to his
face, "We have paid our passage; we have a right on the
boat; and we will do whatever we please." She said she
was so weary and longed to get quiet and rest, but it was

no use to expect they would give her or the [other] passengers a chance to rest. It was too evident this was the
heaven of those who have no love for God and His righteousness.

At this point Ellen White took matters into her own hands.

I made my voice heard from my berth [a nice way to
say that she shouted—and remember that at times she
could project her voice for almost a mile!], begging that
all who considered themselves gentlemen would stop this
unnecessary noise and let those who wanted to sleep have
a chance to do so.

Did it work? She continued: "I was happily surprised that
the noise ceased soon and there was quiet."[11]

It's no wonder the noise got on Ellen's nerves. The weather
was very rough. She wrote: "The day we came on board we had a
general upheaving." Nor was that the first time. On a different
sailing, this time in Europe, she also encountered stormy weather
and reported, "I vomited most earnestly."[12] On the present occa-
sion, after shouting for the rowdy passengers to stop their thundering noise so she could sleep, she said candidly, "For a time it
seemed as though hell itself was let loose."[13]

Ellen White's travel adventures alone would more than fill a
book—maybe two or three books. At times, in different parts of
the world, she was a passenger on eastern and western stage-
coaches, a lumber wagon, a goat cart, a railroad caboose, delivery
wagons, horse-drawn streetcars, a railway boxcar with a crate of
dogs by her side, and even a train engine! The list seems endless.
I've chosen one such travel experience that occurred February 9,
1895, while Ellen was in Australia. Let's imagine the scene before turning to her own words.

Off in the distance comes the faint rumble of horses and a carriage. It steadily grows louder and louder as it comes racing closer. Behind it boils great clouds of dust going in all directions. Rocks, holes, and ruts in the road rock the carriage so violently that passengers have to grab each other or anything else they can get their hands on in order to keep their seats. From time to time the carriage is almost airborne. The driver is trying to outrun an oncoming storm. Massive black clouds loom huge and menacing behind them. And they are getting closer.

The two horses are doing their best, but the storm is fast gaining on them. Dust is everywhere—behind them, in front of them, and even inside the carriage. It swirls around the horses and into everyone's eyes.

Strong winds spring up, causing trees to twist and bend. It rips branches and sends them skyward then slams them down on the road. The horses begin to panic. But in spite of it all, the carriage races on.

Let's pick up the story as Ellen, one of the passengers in the racing carriage, recounted it in her diary.

> The blackness grew deeper. . . . We drove as fast with our colts as we dared. . . . When we were almost home, the fury of the gale struck. . . . Large hail stones began to fall—as large around as a hen's egg. . . . The horses could not keep their footing and twice slipped down on their haunches, for the road was slippery clay.

The youngest of the horses began to panic because "great hail stones . . . were striking her with terrible force." Ellen tells us what happened next.

> I said, "Byron, . . . go to her head; talk to her. Let the horse know it is not you that are beating her." He jumped out, at this suggestion."

Then quickly turning to her friends, May Lacey and Sarah Belden, who were in the carriage with her, Ellen said, "Get out!" The young horse was almost frantic as the women leapt from the carriage.

"She is a strong, sound colt," wrote Ellen, "but broken to the harness only a few months. But she did not kick, neither did she break into a run, but tried to get away from something terrible."

But Ellen was still inside the carriage. May and Sarah came to her rescue.

> They helped me [out], one on one side and one on the other. The wind was blowing with such force that hats were taken from our heads and cushions were blown from the wagon. The heavy carriage cushions, umbrellas, and heavy carriage robes were blown into the field, and were flying in every direction. But we were all out from the carriage, Byron firmly holding the young frightened horse. Had it known its power it could have freed itself from his grasp and torn everything to pieces and killed itself. What a scene!

By this time the three women were fleeing from the horse and running for the house, Ellen being the slowest. Her hat suddenly blew past her and rolled on the ground in front of her. She slowed her pace, managed to scoop up the hat, and kept going! "I grasped my hat in my hand," she wrote, "as it was blowing before me on the ground."

They "were drenched," but their wild dash finally got them to the house and inside. But what about Byron and the colt? Both were still outside, and the hail was still coming down as hard as ever.

Sarah, seeing the terrible fix Byron was in with the terror-stricken horse, "caught up a shawl and ran out again in the fast falling hail." She quickly disappeared from view.

"We could not see them although they were in full sight of the house. The fast falling rain made it impossible to discern anything distinctly." Ellen and May prayed for help.

> Byron said afterwards he did not dare to stir the horses, fearing my horse would become uncontrollable. The colt was finally led close to the paddock fence and Sarah Belden tried to untackle the traces but could not. She then climbed over the fence and held the horse's head over the fence while Byron unhitched the traces and let the horse free. He then led her down to the yard, taking her through the front yard grounds. Sarah Belden came into the house drenched to the skin. After the storm had spent its force, Byron again took the colt and attached her to the wagon and picked up the scattered things which had blown about, and brought them to the house.[14]

Ellen White was God's appointed messenger. Angels appeared to her in visions. But she was also an ordinary woman, dealing with the emergencies and daily demands of life. Sometimes I find it difficult to realize that the exceptional people of the Bible— Noah, Daniel, Peter, Paul, and all the others—were just people like you and me. But they were. They received wonderful, great gifts from God, but they were still just human beings who had to face problems each day as we do. To them, as to us, God gave evidences of His love and care.

On a clear night in northern Italy in the year 1886, Ellen White saw one of those evidences from God. But I'll let her tell about it herself.

> I was looking upon a sight I never expected to see— the starry heavens ablaze with shooting, falling stars,

each leaving a trail of light in its passage across the heavens, and then disappearing. They were crisscrossing in every direction, yet we could not miss any of these jets of light. With emotions I cannot describe we looked for hours upon these shooting, flashing meteors.[15]

She instantly recalled the words of Christ when He said that in the last days of earth's history, "The stars shall fall from heaven" (Matthew 24:29). After watching for hours, she went inside and prepared for bed wondering what all this meant. But she couldn't forget what she had just seen. She had to go outdoors once more to see if the great show in the sky was still there. And it was. Hundreds and hundreds of falling stars were still filling the sky. They were going in all directions as they fell toward earth. She stood in awe.

The amazing adventures of Ellen White were just that—amazing. But never forget for one minute that our lives are no less amazing. We serve the same God. He has not changed. He watches over each one of us as He did Ellen White and those men, women, boys, and girls you read about in the Bible.

So close your eyes for a minute and whisper a prayer. Then count your blessings. Know that God is not only your friend, He loves you. No matter what heartaches and trials you face, life goes on. And when it goes on with God by your side, your little span of life on this earth is indeed truly amazing. It is worth all the effort, for our God is good.

---

1. Ms. 38, 1893, 3.
2. Ms. 88, 1893, 10-12.
3. Ms. 183, 1898, 10, 11.
4. Ms. 24, 1885, 6, 15.
5. Ms. 67, 1886, 4-7.
6. Ms. 32, 1891, 1.
7. Ms. 143, 1904.

8. Ms. 16a, 1885, 2-4, 7, 12-14, 16-19, 22.
9. Ms. 54, 1886, 1-4, 8-10.
10. Ms. 57, 1886, 1, 3, 5.
11. Ms. 76, 1893, 8-10.
12. Ms. 27, 1885, 9-12.
13. Ms. 59, 1895, 5-7.
14. Ibid.
15. Ms. 73, 1886, 1.